Dear Mary,

Thank you for your interest in, and Knowlege of, the Still, Soft Voice!

Shalom, peace,

Dr. Cliff

Avg 25, 2011

Б. Н

It is exceedingly close.

These astonishing breakthroughs
are not hand picked cases.

They are presented in this book
exactly as each happened.

The Still, Soft Voice

We are assured by covenant that any wide-ranging effort
pursued wisely and with friendship is never fruitless.

Hayom Yom ~ 5704
Crown Heights, New York

~

Tinker Bell seems so sad & lonely.
Why does applause help to keep her alive?

As a Child, asking Within
New York, 1954

Knowledge is for the benefit of mankind ...
this is our unifying principle.

An Inaugural Speech to New Students
Rockford College, 1960

Is man's basic nature neutral, bad or good?

Professor's Inquiry to Graduate Students
University of Chicago, 1970

Where do those hypnosis finger movements come from?

As an Adult, asking Within
Chicago workshop, 1981

(See page xxv)

The Still, Soft Voice

The Still, Soft Voice

~

New Frontier of Self

Breaking through to the Inner Core of Consciousness

Clifford K. Brickman

KEMPNER BOOKS

NEW YORK   CHICAGO

Kempner Publishing Co.

Permission@ kempnerpublishing.com

Protection

" Because your innermost thoughts
& feelings are precious."

See page 12

This book introduces the literal reality of a positive inner core
in consciousness. The ideas herein do not replace therapy,
medical or legal advice, yet may help sort out the wise
from the less wise. Those who seek and connect
with the positive core may know integration,
wisdom, understanding and knowledge.

ISBN 0-9671651-1-3

United States of America

Library of Congress Card Number

2011903814

KEMPNER BOOKS

NEW YORK   CHICAGO

Overview

Awakening

I am aware that I'm traveling by myself without a destination throughout
a small town ~ there may be some vague route yet I have no specific direction
of my own

Although I have no intention, no purpose, I observe that I'm going up
and down some hills and some long driveways with buildings about,
into a couple of old homes possibly going through front doors
upstairs and out of a basement or two

Along with the purposelessness is an intriguing ambiance a feeling
of something in the air as I continue along this route through the town
I see no people around ~ yet my overall sense is there may be townsfolk
helping to guide me; I seem to be heading somewhere I know not where

After a time I rather naturally find myself dropped off at the outskirts of
the town to visit a particular area or farm; outside the fence of the farm
is a very quiet meadow; this meadow is still, and special, and even
as I see the mutated animals I realize I am in a hallowed place;
the animals who were "different" .. with elongated necks
and other unusual body forms .. had been brought here
in a caring way by the townspeople I assume

The two-headed calves do not displease nor disgust me as I would have
thought they might; on the contrary, I note how they in particular
belong in this sacred place, and how natural it feels
to see them and to visit this place

While waking, I have a deep appreciation for having been to this place
and about my reactions to it, although it makes no sense at all to me
what it represents; awakening, I am feeling alone and separate.
I could have a lonely feeling but don't; I'm feeling alone
and I'm feeling okay   . . .

~ Early 1989

& why now

You'll be seeing these years after this discovery in 1989. Twenty years are as 20 minutes in the overall scheme of things, yet by usual worldly count it is still a good long time.

Pondering a historical perspective, I'm in a peaceful park, struggling to develop an introduction. It's summer, late afternoon not yet dusk. Some sailboats gently drift by on Lake Michigan. With paper and pen in hand, I'm seated on a low concrete riser, peering out at the quiet lake, here to hopefully pull together some sort of a beginning.

Right behind me, in a continual casual flow, on a crispy rock pathway, are the walkers, joggers, children, parents, dogs; sizes regular, large, teeny and tiny. The myriad of beings crunchily move along, each one with his or her very own signature crunching sound.

Now convening fifteen feet in front of me, on concrete winding down to the water's edge, is a small group of teenagers softly conversing with one another in intriguing melodious tones. Their group garb is hippie-punk if I may so put it, many have colorized hair, some have outlandish oversized bicycles with them. The troupe is quietly engaged in developing some sort of plan of their own.

To my left stand three older, large women speaking together animatedly in their own language. Two of them stroll by me, moving down the ramp closer to the lake and to the group. One remains, seated on the concrete barrier not far from me, intent on reading her book.

The group has been together awhile, quietly meditating ... or in prayer?

Distant sounds of traffic can be heard, yet overall it's quite quiet. The chirping of birds moves into the foreground of my perception, while the young people by the waters continue their meditation. They help my focus as I write.

Early 1989 was an exciting, exhilarating time of discovery. As you now delve into this book, may you feel it and sense this yourself.

The power of these experiences created an indelible impact. As ideas bubbled up, an admonition, "All findings must be chronicled."

Just in case I missed the point, a concordance of events took place at the beginning, a kind of synchrony seen later in many persons' lives after contact with the inner core.

Such an occurrence took place during the initial twenty-eight days, relating to an author-philosopher I'd wondered about for decades, connecting back to my earliest college days and to graduate school; then showing up quite close to home.

Synchronicity bolstered my realization, that first, full recordings must begin immediately. Second, only a book will convey basics and essentials.

But how would I--who had never done such a thing--ever be able to put together a book?

Above, a lone plane ambles across an expanse of clear blue sky. Why the wait to complete this introduction; did I have reservations about its timing? The group at the waters below begins to sing along with guitar, their melodious beat in precise concert with a pat-pat-pat of running shoes against pebbled-path behind me.

It's true I'd attempted to interest publishers during the early 1990s, making the case for psychology interfacing spirituality. *"The public is ready and even thirsting for it,"* I said. They want to know about the knowledge and wisdom literally existing within each and every person.

Meeting in person with a pragmatic editor, I presented my case. I ultimately just showed up in his lobby; and he graciously welcomed me to his office. Enchanting as the meeting was, nevertheless, the idea he did not seem to embrace. I tried but could not seem to convey to him the essence of the inner core--how vital, how real it was, and is.

Was the world of publishing ready for this?

The editor appreciated my perseverance in coming to New York City, and bid me farewell. But perhaps, the idea and my thoughts did reach him. The next year he produced another book, on the general care of the soul.

Barriers to bringing forth *The Still Soft Voice* were undeniable. And this included my reticence about organizing, writing, and cogently conveying a clear understanding. Other blocks to completion were requisite channels of publishing, publicizing and distribution. All of it needed to be in place.

My technical writing and clinical work within a range of psychological contracts were not enough; all of it was preliminary. How was I going to communicate what I was privileged to know about the inner core? The challenge was exponentially greater than anything I'd done in the past.

I'm indebted to private practice for this inner discovery. Truth-seeking and freedom from a strict adherence to any one school of thought, allowed me to freely and genuinely "follow the phenomena" for each patient-client.

The inward focus of private practice offered a protected environment which allowed for nonpartisan exploration. To be separate and apart from distracting and undue influence was critical.

The orientation of inwardness, privacy and protection was essential for discovery, and was an inhibition to my communicating these remarkable events. One premise in investigating the phenomena was to keep it quiet.

Meanwhile, after 25 years as psychotherapist, I found myself immersed, back in school the second half of the 1990s. By 2000 with the additional, more tangible perspective of a doctor in holistic medicine, moving into the biological and relatively more outward realms, perhaps I'd be better able to carry this message from the inside to the outside.

Pioneers involved will likely recall many of the words of the inner core. One reason for a time lapse since 1989 is for the needs of clients-patients-persons to more fully metabolize these significant inner happenings.

Actual identities will remain protected unless otherwise authorized. All are invited to be in touch about their experiences with and reflections on the inner core over these decades.

For the greatest credibility, utmost accuracy is maintained. No embellishment is added nor any artistic license taken. After the initial three attempts, all of the breakthroughs were tape-recorded.

The time has come to share a wondrous phenomenon. This realm is precious and certainly we need to keep in mind appreciation for all those involved; and to see this subject not as a momentary fad, instead to understand it for what it is, an opening.

The teenagers finish up their gathering. They move up the ramp with easy grace and increasing sound, with their double-size bicycles in tow as they leave, duos and trios bantering with one another, some doing wheelies, and then disbanding ... quietly moving on.

I look out at the lake. Dusk is approaching. Now only two people are left, myself and the woman reading her book.

It has become ever so quiet.

I've often pondered the consequences of this venture; I envision it as expediting an expansion of reality as thought to be. Looking back with amusement, we will see how narrow-minded and constricted, how xenophobic or autophobic, we once were.

A new realization will become more clear, the world is not flat, and a watershed of psycho-social ramifications will spring forth.

My aim is for your great benefit, as you resonate with these ideas and thoughts, as you find this good place within your Self. May you know the wonders waiting within, now venturing forth.

C.K.B.

Aug. 26, 2010

& who is responsible

Contemplating how this writing will measure up to the subject matter it presents, it won't ~ how could it even approach the magnificence of the Still, Soft Voice.

There is a saving grace, and that is, the Core speaks for itself. My aim is to present its words precisely, neither adding nor subtracting anything. To the extent this can be accomplished, I hold no reservations.

Welcome to the book!

It is crafted with *flow* in mind to make it easier to absorb. No matter what is your style of reading--whether front-to-back straight through, or back-to-front, or finding which page jumps out at you--please be sure to read with special care its *words in bold*.

For these are the articulations of the Still Soft Voice.

Its words are presented verbatim.

If you do approach this as bibliographic Self-development, reading first the discovery and breakthrough chapters, reflecting on these as a process of unfolding, may be a useful course to pursue.

Enter in peace ~ come out in peace.

Take it one step at a time.

"Who is responsible" goes a step further.

The next day upon awakening, another idea showed up. Such is the surprise, delight or wonder as it goes from nothing into something:

When distraction, procrastination and delay occur, we usually do not know why. When positive flow occurs, obstacles evaporate or are more readily overcome. As writing becomes easier, we must ask,*"Why is this so?"*

I Am is in the picture, as negatives are off to the side and out of the way--*ego* can be cooperative, there to be of help when invited.

As blockage is better understood and overcome, a fuller awareness develops; one's projects and life become more in sync with Innermost energies. Intentionality is heightened and purified. Good things can and do take place.

❖

Table of CONTENTS

The vessel shatters,
*   the divine spark shines through.*

PRELUDE

SHATTERED VESSELS & BLAZING LIGHT

~

1985

September 23, 1985

The Holy Day's meditation was curiously appealing. As a modern person and psychotherapist, I didn't understand, yet liked it.

The poetic notions gave me a sense of satisfaction--enough to go back, copy it down and carefully file it away for years. Why was I drawn to poetry I didn't quite get? What I felt was a consolation.

The page of verse showed up in a hand-stapled booklet for New Years services on campus at University of Chicago, my professional base *CIRCA* 1970. In choosing religious services located near my educational roots, I went there to seek comfort and peace during some challenging high holy days.

It was 1985 and this was a homecoming to the Hyde Park campus where I studied during the late sixties. Those religious services held by students at my old University of Chicago campus were soothing to me after sudden, unceremonious cutoff in love. The verses offered solace for emotional distress.

The Meditation showed up later in my papers. I decided to present it here as written, in the spirit of my own journey just as it unfolded. This is not meant to take anything at all away from clinical science, nor to dissuade anyone from his or her own specific journey. On the contrary, experiencing the core heightens appreciation of true spiritual expression within the many faiths of this world, not only one's own.

In reality the inner core belongs to each and every person whether of one faith or of another, or if having none. [1]

---

[1] *.. if none, what else have you?*

Meditation

We pause in reverence before the gift of self,

The vessel shatters, the divine spark shines through,
And our solitary self becomes a link
     in Israel's golden chain.
For what we are, we are by sharing.
And as we share
We move toward the light.

We pause in reverence before the mystery
     of a Presence,

The near and far reality of God.
Not union, but communion is our aim.
And we approach the mystery
With deeds. Words lead us to the edge of action.
But it is deeds that bring us closer to the
     God of light.

We pause in terror before the human deed:
The cloud of annihilation, the concentrations
     for death,
The cruelly casual way of each to each.
But in the stillness of this hour
We find our way from darkness into light.

May we find our life so precious
But that we cannot but share it with the other,
That light may shine brighter than a thousand
     suns,
With the presence among us of the God of light.

As I write initially in 1993, a memory from 1985 pops to mind to surprise me. During the New Year's service in spite of my training and background, I actually posed specific *questions* to the One Above.

In my personal and professional philosophy at the time, conjecture about God was allowable and acceptable ... but *"talking" with Him ?!* Perhaps, only in one's heart of hearts, but other than prayers recited in monotone unison, shouldn't this be the province of fundamentalists?

With the values of the 1960s, a liberal childhood of the 1940-50s, and psychotherapy training of the 1970-80s, I wasn't a fundamentalist. Circumstances of heavy emotion provided the impetus. The personal relationship broken three days earlier countered any cultural shyness or reticence.

A freshly wounded heart spoke for itself.

The questions asked by me were simple and few, relating to love and relationship. Answers were concise and to the point, mostly "yes," "no," or "you will see." I did not always get a specific response. These answers were perceived by me as coming from imagination. Whatever, the responses held a ring of truth and a sense of comfort.

"Are these answers coming from in my imagination?," I wondered "or *by way* of my imagination?" How could one really know. There was no way to answer this question at that time. The idea passed--but embedded in that momentary muse was an embryonic discovery.

At the moment of this sentence in 1993, I became aware the idea expressed above was also a *question!* Had I unknowingly been given an inkling of the *answer*? [2]

---

[2] *Only from a perspective eighteen years later: perhaps the verses of meditation themselves introduced a part of the answer.*   -2007

Questions: they're useful in individual, family therapy, in gestalt imagery, and in hypnotherapy and psychotherapy.

Since early years as a psychotherapist, I provided a transactional version of gestalt psychotherapy. Therapeutic questions were directed from the "inner Child" of a specific age to its "inner Parent."

My aim was to identify torment, and pinpoint any disturbances in the introjected parent-child relationships, to resolve inter-generational trauma and upset of emotions and perceptions. [3]

I became acquainted in 1981 with (but not drawn to using) hypnotic questioning in trance, via finger movement responses for "yes," "no" or "I don't want to answer."

This is known as ideomotor questioning. From when I first observed it, I recall a question of my own which even then felt significant, *"From where do these responses come?"*

As to thinking about core, I studied body psychotherapies including the concept of a "bioenergetic core." In a therapist training group, it was often asked, "How is your core today?" A good question, yet to me it felt too glib and lacking reality for useful application.

~

My own questions at services in 1985 were not quite as they had been elsewhere (in gestalt therapy, in visualizations nor clinical hypnosis). They were especially heartfelt, even spiritual; and they were all mine.

After high holidays, and with a gradual easing of those intense feelings, I filed away those poetic verses, its words all but forgotten.

---

[3] *I think of this as becoming increasingly "hypnosis-free" by resolving "family-trance" zones to obtain greater freedom and clarity of mind and heart.*   *November 2008*

Social Landscape
Ides of March 1989

Berlin Wall was a wall,
Soviet Union an empire,
& Tian'anmen a square.

AN OPENING

Three years & seven months later ...

~

Cosmic Landscape
22 March 1989

4581 Asclepius, 300 meters wide
misses Earth by six hours.

Break through to the Inner Core

1989

" For it is exceedingly close, to you.. "

The Pioneers

Discovery

Inside

We are each other.

<1>

Myron

On The Deep

April 11th, 1989

I am on the deep Inside.

He is everything else.

Name	Age	Occupation	Inner contact	Prior therapy
Myron	26	Financial securities	4-11-89	2.5 months

Myron was the consummate outside salesman. And he stayed worried nearly all the time.

He was pessimistic about his job and his life.

As Myron put it, he was "out of touch with feelings," and did "not function well with customers nor people in general." When first describing his concerns, he offhandedly commented, *"It's like something else there, not me."* Without more to say, he only knew this was an impediment.

First, is a condensed picture of our work together.

The outside world of expectations and performance was all-important to Myron. He felt under a constant and unrelenting pressure to perform, which was fine with him! He believed that approach was the best approach, and the only way to be.

He expected performance from therapy--more to the point, from the therapist, meaning me. I assented reluctantly.

I believed it critically important to offer psychotherapy first, and hypnotherapy second. His priorities differed. Myron saw me as hypnotherapist first, and actually, as hypnotist period. His demand was hypnosis; he was a frank taskmaster about it.

As psychotherapy was encouraged, Myron lobbied for more hypnosis. While accommodating his insistence, I taught him self-hypnosis as well. My campaign for therapy in general continued without an effect.

After two months of unrelenting hypnosis, something began to develop. We were pursuing a curious and novel hypnotic incident--that is, a *positive* response for Myron! He bestowed accolades upon me about it, even while complaining how short-lived his response.

6

"Now do it again," he implored.

Despite his demand to repeat it, instead, we developed a mutual curiosity about the *why* and the *how* it had worked out as well as it had for him.

After investigating, I was able to find what was sought.

It turned out there *was* something else there, seemingly not him. In *a slow* and *un*-pressurized manner, *it* pinpointed a distinction,

> " *I* am the *inside*. *He* is the *outside*. "

In contrast to the pressurized Myron seen up until that moment, *this or it* clearly and carefully advised a distinction,

> " *Don't ever push me*. "

Overall, its manner and style were a complete turnabout. Myron seemed suddenly pressure-free. I experienced some relief myself, even with the heavier, cautionary statement. With my prime focus on the procedure itself, I didn't have time to be shocked or overly surprised, yet realized this was in fact a something quite different.

This "Inside" effortlessly and precisely clarified the contextual whole problem, brought a two-year old Mirey into the picture, and brought out a small child's trauma of abandonment.

In twenty years of explorations, I hadn't seen anything like this ...an "Inside" so incongruous with an "Outside."

Next is how this discovery came to be.

At the Beginning.

Myron came in for therapy late January 1989 at 26 years of age. When we first said hello in the waiting area, his demeanor was extrovertive, as if a salesman, with friendly façade, on a business call. His energetic congeniality seemed incongruous with coming in to see someone for therapy.

As we moved into my office, and after I closed the heavy soundproofed door, Myron resolutely maintained the salesman aura and presence. He presented me a business card, spoke on finance, and inquired after my general financial picture.

His exuberant friendliness seemed like a veneer but it soon became clear. This was no façade. For Myron this was surely the real thing. He had come to therapy because he was aware something was wrong ,,, he did not connect with people and thought others sensed something lacking in him. He was alienated, worried about his job, and his desire was therefore, as he put it, to become a better overachiever!

During the first session, Myron described a "pressure all the time, physically around the crown of his head, emotionally an apprehension and nervousness." When around other people, symptoms intensified, and he felt an increase in blood pressure and heart rate.

"The _Real me_ is an overachiever," he proclaimed, "but there is something else there--a _Not me_ which alters everything. It blocks me from being me, and people perceive me to be more apprehensive and less outgoing. And it's all below my ability to control it."

He thought of this "Not me" as an impediment to his greater achievement. Although my saying it had no effect, I interpreted this as a barrier to his freedom

Myron saw himself as coming from a happy family, yet he was not. He grew up unhappy, depressed and without friends.

"The problem," he emphasized, "is *not* with my family; it is only with *me*, myself."

Myron had few memories of childhood yet was told by parents about a dramatic personality change in him, a shift occurring when his mother was hospitalized for complications, some three or four months after giving birth to Michael's sibling.

His father was often away to see his wife, but being so young, two-year-old Mirey could not get to see his mom. "From a happy gregarious explorer, I became a withdrawn little hermit."

The family could not ameliorate his persistent problems nor was any therapy sought. "Why not?," I queried. Later asking his father, Myron conveyed the explanation, "Therapists back then did more harm than good."

Attempts to explore nuance in family dynamics were thwarted. According to Myron, it was quite simple: the family "could not do any wrong." He remained steadfast in his position. Even any subtle challenges were met with great indignation. Usual therapy options were restricted due to his protests, with an implied caution to tread lightly on any subject of family.

Months later, he revealed he'd been in a prior therapy but the therapist "tried to turn me against my family." He had dropped out.

Myron had not much positive to say about himself. Although his pessimism weighed heavily upon him, his goal was not related to his emotions. He simply desired greater achievement.

He approached his therapy with high performance expectations, and particularly directed at me. My aims here were to lower his stress and to promote some introspection, but a laid-back reflective psychotherapy this was not going to be.

I had been a clinical therapist for about twenty years. While I did provide active modalities as hypnosis, my basic allegiance was to a person-centered approach; meaning, its focus and its foundation are the patient's perceptions and experience.

Power for change resides within the person, that I believed, although additional technical modalities could be employed.

My version of hypnotherapy was person-centered, and not the old-style authoritarian. My own goal was to go further than modern permissive hypnosis, i.e., to *follow the phenomena.*

While in graduate school I wrote, "When is a Gardener a Mechanic?" The gist of it was organismic growth, and yet also, technical intervention as needed.

The persons of client and therapist are significant in therapy, and the client more than therapist "sets the agenda and carries the ball."

To engage Myron as a person, meant connecting with his selfhood, and his feelings. Interactional psychotherapy, I felt, was critically necessary, not just plain-and-simple hypnosis.

Myron was not interested in the vagaries of intrinsic growth. At times people came to me primarily for hypnosis, and this is what he sought--to the maximum. Despite my encouragement otherwise, and his humoring me, what he really had in mind was exclusively hypnosis, being *done to* him and *not by* him.

I had to acclimatize my frustration to his relentless pressure and his unshakable expectation, "The therapist not the patient must carry the ball."

Myron acknowledged therapy may take time...and he was going to give *me* the time. Was he politely placating me?

We agreed to balance technical hypnosis with talk therapy, but after any session without hypnosis he felt empty, and even cheated. I was losing my campaign for Myron's emotional participation.

Despite the continuing tension of our differing viewpoints, his persistence for hypnosis was accommodated, with an outcome of "not much happening." Nevertheless, we plowed ahead with *his* technical hypnosis and *my* person-centered philosophy. I still hoped against hope to *follow the phenomena.*

Embryonic Discovery.

Ten weeks of continuous hypnosis later, something did occur. An unusual reaction took place the end of a session, *and* for a day afterwards.

For Myron this was a radical departure--it was *positive!*

He actually had a good day. He felt "wonderful" for *a whole day*. He did not know why; he just did. He knew it was somehow from the hypnosis; and now he wanted to "recreate that wonderful feeling of having no problems and being okay!"

With Myron using such an unusual adjective as wonderful, was this a glimmer of hope? Despite instantaneous pressure to redo it!, this was a relief, at least momentarily, for me.

Complaining the reaction was so short-lived, Myron entailed, "Do it again!" He believed the hypnotherapist knew precisely what had occurred, and thus from his point of view it was quite simple. "Just repeat it."

It wasn't so simple. Myron's reaction reminded me of moments of bliss: the more one's desire to grasp onto these tightly, the more fleeting they can be.

Technically, could this even be repeated?

Perhaps his interlude from stress was based on mobilization of hope. How genuine a phenomenon might this be or not. Was it something beyond a placebo effect?

Michael wanted answers from me, but neither of us knew why the good response. To be able to answer questions about hypnotic outcome, I felt, there was no viable alternative other than to track it back to a cause.

Precisely what had happened; and how come?

The previous session in hypnosis we had "FIXED THE SEAL," a procedure especially useful for someone with high hypnosis abilities. After considering and planning for weeks, Myron was looking forward to it.

"FIXING THE SEAL" gives a hypnotic suggestion to safeguard the person from any hypnosis other than what he or she wants and needs therapeutically,[4]

> " *NO ONE WILL BE ABLE TO HYPNOTIZE YOU UNLESS YOU WANT TO BE OR NEED TO BE, UNLESS YOU TRUST THE PERSON DOING SO, AND KNOW HE OR SHE IS QUALIFIED.*
>
> *BECAUSE THAT PERSON IS DEALING WITH YOUR INNERMOST THOUGHTS AND FEELINGS, AND THEY ARE PRECIOUS.* "

This protection may help seal vulnerability to unwanted influence. It can be useful. At the conclusion of his procedure, Myron was exuberant.

"I'm looking forward to becoming the master of my own destiny!"

---

[4] *"FIXING THE SEAL" as developed by Dr. F. J. MacHovec, conveyed and provided in 1981 at a hypnotherapy workshop, Atlanta, Georgia.*

Hope and positive expectation are critical but based upon so sudden this uncharacteristic optimism, I had concerns about rebound effects. Could this live up to Myron's expectations?

Based upon his temperament, it was slightly startling to see in our next session this "wonderful feeling" in fact having endured for a whole day!

Even thinking Myron developed a boundary clarification, and thus felt better, it was unlikely we could do the same again.

The Seal theoretically fixed, to repeat it again, could diminish its impact. Instead, might we possibly learn from this occurrence to move beyond an impasse?

We refocused on technical aspects of the hypnosis. Reviewing the basics in *Fixing the Seal*, a phrase popped out for Myron,

"YOUR INNERMOST THOUGHTS AND FEELINGS ARE PRECIOUS"

Could these words have something to do with it?

Although displeased about my not wanting to instantly repeat the procedure, Myron did agree to exploratory hypnosis based on his reaction to the words above.

I reconstruct this hypnosis session from my notes *April 6, 1989*. My aim was to look for *"something inside"* that might help with *"precious innermost feelings."*

We did in fact find, not the ordinary inner Child or Parent but rather a different inside part. And it was negative! Whatever it was we found, according to Myron afterwards, it did *not* want him to be successful.

A sudden concern arose, *"You'll leave me!"* An inner response was, *"No stupid, I won't."* What this not an unfriendly support?

At the conclusion of the ten to fifteen minutes of hypnosis, and back awake, right before leaving the office, Myron felt the whole "inner exploration thing" had been a waste of his time.

13

Myron was more pessimistic than ever, highly upset about "getting nowhere." I wasn't happy myself about this rebound reaction. Could this have been predicted it to him? A gloomy situation was devolving. Additionally, he happened to mention, he was planning to soon take a rock-climbing trip.

Based on intensity and critical necessity, something needed to come to mind! Myron was waiting for me, expectantly.

How to intervene...what to say to Myron right now?

On an intuitive impulse,[5] I confronted Myron,

"If this was a negative part, wouldn't there have to be a positive part? If we've found a negative self-helper, wouldn't there have to be a positive self-helper?! ~ if only for balance!"

Myron summarily rejected my assertion. He responded, *"This is the only self-helper! And it is negative!!"*

~

Over the weekend I traveled east to New York, for a family gathering and a renewal of perspective and energy. On Monday April 10, I took the Staten Island ferry with a car and drove throughout my childhood locale, age two to ten.

Later in the evening I flew back to the Midwest. My travels throughout the New York city--and revisiting many childhood memories--had otherworldly qualities to it. The whole trip held special meaning to me, kind of like a pilgrimage and definitely an inspiration.

~

The next day back in Chicago, with Myron in a hypnotic trance, my hope and aim was to find a *positive* self-helper. My image of the straight staircase where he was typically directed, instantaneously morphed into a *circular* staircase.

---

[5] *An intuition ~ and thought developing incrementally over years. The idea had been incubating based in part on clinical theory.*

A Breakthrough.

April 11, 1989

Myron was in a deep hypnotic trance, his forearm remaining up, his eyes closed. There at the bottom of the circular staircase was a something, seemingly different. I asked some questions.

Words came back s-l-o-w-l-y and deliberately. [6]

WHO AM I TALKING WITH?

" *I am the Inside ~ he is the outside.* "

HOW DO YOU RELATE TO MYRON?

" *He's unhappy. I am still Okay.* "

WHERE ARE YOU LOCATED?

" *I'm on the Deep Inside. He's everything else.* "

This mode was a diametric contrast to Myron seen up to then. It was dramatically different; and it was not pressurized at all.

Thought was objective and without high emotionality. It felt neither dependent nor demanding. The voice was clear and deep.

Without a question, it secerned a declaration,

" *Don't push me ... don't ever pressure me.* "

---

[6] From notes taken during hypnotic session.

This Inside clarified problems, went into a childhood trauma and the lifelong reactions to it, bringing in two-year-old inner Myron into the process.

I asked more questions, those Myron had for so long.

MYRON FEELS THERE IS A BLOCK HERE.
 WHAT IS THE BLOCK ABOUT?
" *Not meant as a block.* "

THEN WHAT?
" *To keep people from hurting us.* "

WHAT DO YOU MEAN?
" *Other people can hurt us.*

HOW?
 In the beginning of life ...
  We were left alone. Long times. Terrified.
   very little ... *always looking out the window.*

HOW DID IT FEEL?
  Wanting to cry   All the time ~ cry.
  The grandmother helped. "

WHAT IS YOUR NAME?
  my name is Myer----real little - - too little.
  have to protect ourself ...

WHAT DO YOU DO?

> *... don't let people get close ~ so can't hurt us.*
>
> *... parents ~ no big deal   Other side ~ he likes them.*

HOW DOES THIS HAPPEN?

> *I control everything . . I have to, protecting.*
>
> *Almost died once   ~   we were left alone.*
>
> *. . love other side.*

~

My basic concern was, what was it I'd sought, and what was it we had just found?

Whatever this was, it provided fundamentals:

An Outside.

> " *He's on the outside.*
>
> *He's unhappy .. me, I'm still OK.* "

An Inside.

> " *I'm on the inside.*
>
> *I make him feel pain .. not on purpose* "

A Boundary for Survival.

> " *I'm not going out.*
>
> *I control it ~ he does it.* "

And a Key Point.

> " *..would do things to help him !* "

Back awake, Myron described what it was like for him,

" I watched and heard him communicate with you.

I couldn't say anything.

He was in control. "

~

" Same name, same person, or same being,

but previously never the twain shall meet. "

<u>What was this</u>?

Myron reported plainly,
"It had a mind of its own."

To him this was intriguing. To me it was sort of stunning.

This was such a stark divergence from Myron's character. During the hypnosis, an inherent temperament of tremendous pressurization had all but evaporated; and seemingly it was replaced entirely with something else.

Given Michael's tenacious task orientation, what was this new, evenhanded approach? This suddenly understanding even wise mode possessed warmth and care. Out of nowhere, not having been seen nor felt before by Myron: how was this mode even a possibility here?

This "Mind" held awareness with independence of thought. Myron heretofore glorified pressure, but this mode would not accept it at all. This extraordinary and salubrious temperament seemed at ease and in sync with itself, and beyond itself.

Considering Possibilities.

Different explanations flashed through my mind. Categories did not fit particularly well: ego states, dissociation, post-traumatic stress, multiplicity; simply high hypno-abilities ... ?

Diagnostic thinking kicked into play. This is the type of thought that can sometimes be useful particularly after sessions. In this context it was not easy to determine anything especially helpful.

Was it multiplicity of personality? Could be, but most likely not. So far as we both knew, this presentation had not interacted ever before with any external environment. From what I had observed in two-and-a-half months, Myron was always in control. Other than initially mentioning, "like something else there," his usual character maintained a constricted range of pressurized thought, feeling and action.

I scoured other possibilities.

What about a factitious disorder? Might this supposed "Inside" be made-up? This too was unlikely because there was no purpose, no secondary gain to it. And with a tenacious hard-line personality, how could he readily bring forth a relaxed and wise approach that conveyed warmth and care?

How could this presentation transcend Michael's character and functioning? Could it be his limitations were disingenuous in the first place? Over the years I had occasionally seen self-appointed veterans never having been in the military yet sporting Navy Seal caps.[7] Each had factitious troubles: playing loosely with the truth, with self-esteem hunger and a profound need to impress.

This didn't apply either. If one is able to outperform one's own constraints, why be in therapy at all, to feign problems? to fool a therapist? There was no disability claim nor anyone to impress.

---

[7] *Civilians, not knowing how to swim.*

Therapist expectations.

Was this an adaptation to a hypnotherapist expectation? Even with olden-style authoritarian hypnotherapy, it would not happen the way this just did. Hypnotherapy can bring about symptomatic relief and some behavioral change, but it doesn't produce a personality transplant like this one.

My style of hypnotherapy was permissive, person-centered and not very directive. I was motivated as therapist to respond to Myron's critical need but was there a prior expectancy?[8] Up to this time nothing like it had occurred in my practice. I had sought something, to help Myron at a desperate juncture.

Did the intensity of need become the father of invention? I felt a strong need to act in behalf of Myron...to explore, to find *any*thing in contrast to pervasive ego-syntonic negatives. The motif or energy sought by me was in a direct contrast to his conundrum and to his perceptual framework.

In theory I introduced a "positive self-helper,"[9] but Myron had not previously accepted my aims nor any of my ideas. On the contrary, he humored me while adamantly embracing his own notions.

And not to forget, Myron himself initially had a vague idea about, "*Something else there, not me.*"

In twenty years of psychotherapy exploration, I'd never seen anything like this--an inside so incongruous with a basic character.

This inner aspect had never communicated with an external environment. Myron had always run the show.

---

[8] *These days I perceive a specific "intentionality" as helpful and crucial. In early 1989 that concept and action was muted, only developing.*   *3/2005*

[9] *Or, the positive was there all along, cloaked in negativity.*   *11-20-2008*

Given Myron's tenacity of personality, it was unlikely he could produce this; would he enjoy giving up his coveted control?

This inner state had a ring of truth to it, but what was it really? This new development required follow-up: to look for any useful benefits for him, and to look out for any detriments or difficulties with this ostensibly powerful energy.

As in One.

Although nothing fit in pigeonhole fashion; and assuming this to be an anomaly specific to Myron, still, somewhat subliminally I pondered, what about with others .. *as in one so with all?*

Each person is an individual like no other, yet I've believed we share commonalties with all others even if we think we don't. [10] What seems unusual or abnormal can teach us something about our biology or psychology and bring forth universal meanings.

Miraculous happenings with every embryo exist within each one of us. Differences exist and we are so very much the same. In the realm of consciousness we hold essentials in common.

All of this might be applicable only to Myron.

Or how may these dynamics apply to others?

Summary.

In this first inner core occurrence, Myron's "greater mind" poignantly clarified a childhood abandonment, brought out an insecure two-year old, and provided care and protection.

---

[10] *Especially when we think we don't.*   *5-14-2005*

This "Mind" possessed superb understanding and a uniquely refined thought process--a stark contrast to the distortions and defense maneuvers typically observed, not only with Myron.

Evidently, this one was not defensive, even with its singular cautionary declaration; was it free of distortion or projection, possibly even having and needing no defense at all?

It was thus far very wise and straightforward.

With repeat experiences it became increasingly clear to me. This was like being with a therapist's therapist or consultant's consultant. Whatever this was, it was like talking with no other.

What's next.

My basic concerns were about risks, gains and applications.

1. Will this help Myron? might it hurt him?
2. What will develop next with Myron?
3. Might this apply to others?

It occurred to me, however this may go, it might be a good idea to audio tape sometime soon.

SEQUENCE

STEP-BY-STEP: Stress-reducing treatment techniques were supplied at Myron's imperative. When each did not satisfy his requirements, we took a next logical step, while keeping to a basic therapy tenet, "Follow the patient's lead and need." Therapy was initially supportive, later moved to more dynamic explorations.

After two months of therapy,

1. March 21: Hypnotherapy, Analeptic Circle of Progress; discussed *"Fixing the Seal;"* and a prescription for self-hypnosis.

2. March 28: Hypnosis to decrease social discomfort.

3. April 4: Hypnotherapy, *Fixing the Seal* "to safeguard the innermost thoughts and feelings, because they are precious." Very positive yet temporary response, we knew not why.

4. April 6: Hypnotherapeutic exploration, finding an "inner self-helper?" Myron perceived it as negative. 11

5. April 11: Hypnotherapeutic exploration to seek a possibly positive inner helper. Found! ~ "The Inside."

6. May 4: First tape-recording of Myron's Inner Core.

---

[11] *Was it negative? Eighteen years later, I understand it differently.*   *2-03-2007*

Egg with Spikes

In control, when I need to be.

<2>

John G.

Defend Yourself

April 12th, 1989

Forever ~ a long time.

Name	Age	Occupation	Inner contact	Prior therapy
John	42	Service	4-12-89	33 months

*J*ohn despised his inner child.

   Three decades of self-disdain would not let up.

John was extraordinarily verbal. His mode of friendliness appealed to others. They liked him; he did not.

A forty-two year old Vietnam veteran, he was twelve years in post-military therapy, now including 33 months with me. After being referred by his previous therapist, despite all their and our PTSD/psychotherapy treatment, a critical childhood trauma could not be dislodged.

The son of a single mother, he grew up in a poor neighborhood adjacent to the University of Chicago. He felt inadequate in comparison to his "intellectually gifted lab-school friends," one of whom became a major television personality.

In his self-expression, it would not be difficult to visualize John as a popular television personality himself. To this day, he laughingly scoffs when I repeat this.

John was the first person with *low* hypno-ability to attempt to reach the inner core. Someone in the lower-third hypnosis potential is usually *high* in cognition and *low* in visualization. Still, we hoped hypnosis might help move beyond his verbal talent and intellectual defense; these were challenging.

During the course of therapy, hypnosis had been employed ten times for smoking and eating but with minimal results. Our hypnotic focus, this time, would be on the Inside. John was receptive to the idea, and he resonated with a "separate part" we'd attempt to reach. John added, it was the "powerful part" from which he was "cut off and in conflict."

This new thought was promising somehow. After hypnosis, however, John was disappointed; he felt certain we had *not* found that powerful part, not at all.

26

April 12, 1989

John went into a deeper hypnotic trance than previously. A request was made to the inner part John just described.

CB: I'D LIKE TO SPEAK TO THE OTHER PART, POWERFUL PART...

*There were no clear responses. John was not able
to say much at all, and he could not move at all.
There were a few mumbled, nearly inaudible words.*

"You're going to hurt me."

" *Spikes...defend yourself...*

"I tell him what to do.

In control, when I need to be.

Forever ~ long time. "

Only after awakening, could John say anything. He did report sadness, anger, a traumatic fight in grammar school, and a thought about defending himself from the outside world.

Too much weight loss would attract too much attention, in brief *"Too slim would be too close."* [12]

John's basic thought was the hypnosis did not work at all, but as an afterthought he described an image.

"An Egg thing -- a smooth shape, with Spikes for defense. There was a perpendicular line through the egg ... with a body on the other side."

And that was it, no more. Focusing attention on the spiked egg, John thought we had run into his usual defensive block. He was quite clear: we had *not* made contact with that "powerful part," and the attempt had failed.

---

[12] *This may have emanated from the core.*   *11-29-2008*

Neither John nor I gave up on his psychotherapy of course, but we did not pursue further hypnosis for a month.

We continued to plod along.

❖

Reviewing original notes years later, it became clear to me. [13] Neither of us had considered the deeper meaning of the egg nor the source energizing it nor what was illuminating it.

What did the egg represent & what put it there? Whether from inside the egg, certain answers were provided. Unbeknownst to us, we had heard from the inner core. [14] [15]

This was to be better understood later.

The Inner core had indeed provided for John and for me,
~ Direction[16] ~ Prescription[17] ~ and Care.[18]

And, imbedded "in the egg" may have been,
~ a Timeline.[19]

Early the following year we found success, reaching a clear dialogue with what was sought.

---

[13] Retrospective realization was 16 years after.
                                                          4-01-2005

[14] From vantage point 16 years later: A key phrase, **'Forever~long time.'** stands out. It resonates with what was to become a theme.
                                                          3-09-2005

[15] ...and from *above* the egg. *See Postscript Dec 26, 1989.*
                                                          5-16-2005

[16] *See Postscript:* We did move ahead, gradually in positive direction.
                                                          3-09-2005

[17] Meaning of *'defend yourself,'* the Egg and its spikes, would become more clear. John was plagued by effects of a brutal childhood fight.
                                                          3-25-2005

[18] ...Carefully and gently...as in *walking on eggshells!*
                                                          3-25-2005

[19] Apr 12, 1989 to Jan 16, 1990. 9-months, a gestation period?
                                                          3-28-2005

POSTSCRIPT

Timeline

Hypnosis sessions,
1989.

April 12 - Egg with spikes for defense.

May 10 - Vague "inner child playing hide-and-seek."

June 21 - Slight encouragement ~ to contact the Egg.
At home, as he slept John was forcefully
confronted by his late mother and sister,

" Choose life or choose death! "

~

Hugging his inner child, remarkably
he finally felt a peace and serenity.

John chose life.

Dec. 26 - The Egg "illuminated from above."

1990.

Jan. 16 - Direct dialogue with the Inner core.

E yes wide open

I had access to a deeper level.

– Robert

<3>

Robert

I Am

April 13th, 1989

An avenue coming out of my heart.

Name	Age	Occupation	Inner contact	Prior therapy
Robert	29	Editor	4-13-89	14 months
			5-10-89	

Robert outwardly appeared to have it all.

He worked in a fine publishing house. He and his lady friend were smart, attractive and doing well, and yet he was stressed and puzzled about not feeling quite centered.

Reserved with an equanimity and reasoned balance, Robert could not pin down a certain self-consciousness; and he found this to be distressing.

For fourteen months, psychotherapy progressed effectively even enjoyably while some of his discomfort diminished.

In addition to talk therapy, we utilized gestalt, transactional, script, bioenergetics. The sole hypnotic procedure the first year was a brief profile indicating a positive potential, yet a lower response. Robert wasn't drawn to hypnotherapy and we did not pursue it.

Robert was in therapy partly through encouragement of his longtime lady friend. Therapy had been useful, but now with diminishing returns, we were considering termination at least for the time being.

As a couple though, they felt something was still missing and thus sought a continuation of therapy.

With renewed motivation, in February the hypnotic profile was performed again, with somewhat better responsiveness. A brief hypnosis session took place, and then another in March. At each session, Robert visualized three successive screens or channels *One, Two and Three.* Details follow.

1 Problem channel, 2 Relaxation, 3 Solution channel.

The two fifteen-minute sessions were nearly identical. The first time, *Screen 1:* family concern (the second time, flashing), *Screen 2:* pond by the seashore in the country (the second time, a pond in the woods with pine trees and a *sun*).

Screen 3 was both times humorous and fuzzy. First time was "a LABORATORY quick" with a "Mr. Science," said with a laugh. Second time, again was Mr. Science and the laboratory. Robert called it "a corny cliche." He thought it was going nowhere.

To try to provide more understanding I suggested Robert add, *"a Screen four, the Meaning channel."*

Screen 4 only showed a single word, *"**guide**"* [20]

Robert didn't know the meaning of the *Meaning screen*. Neither did I. Without more ideas, [21] we took it no further.

~

Again, as therapy was completing, a mistake occurred, all mine. Reliable times are central to therapy but twice to my dismay I had nearly forgotten his appointment; and then a unique occurrence, I actually missed a session.

I left my office and did not see it in my appointment book until three days later. Robert had not left any message.

As soon as I realized my unintentional neglect, I immediately phoned him. Robert handled it graciously, and I wondered aloud, "What might be the meaning of this oversight!"

I asked of myself, *"What* could I possibly have been thinking?" Pondering these dynamics, I thought about the current veracity of our therapeutic alliance.

Was something lacking here, or might this be connected to our saying good-bye?

---

[20]The first time I noticed this was in editing now 16 years later, after an intuition, *"Look up the prior hypnosis!"* There it was in hypnosis notes March 8, 1989 a month *before* discovering it, one word--***Guide***. *3-29-2005*
   ...and before I'd ever thought of a Mr. Science laboratory. *10-06-2008*
[21] ~ until revisiting, then including, the 3 Screens details. *5-18-2005*

A remaining issue was Robert developing an even greater sense of trust in himself for his future. Quite likely, there was still unfinished business about this trust. Was there possibly more to address before parting?

In person on *April 5*, I apologized again and charged no fee. On an intuition I promised to "make it up to him." Although my pledge was surprising even to me, given the circumstances, it felt correct and right; somehow I intended to honor it.

But how?

With this jolt to therapy in mind, I suggested for next week we do deeper hypnotic work. Robert was interested, and agreed to go ahead with it the next session.

Between the time of my pledge and of Robert's next session, an inkling developed on my part about *what* to actually seek. Robert did rely on me, although at the time I knew preciously little about what could or would occur.

Our therapy alliance of fourteen months was secure enough I felt, to handle it. Robert was ready, and because I had to be, so was I.

April 13, 1989

Comfortably seated on the couch, his feet on the footstool, Robert faced forward. I moved to sit off to his right as I do.

We begin.

"Eyes closing ..closing.. completely closed ..elbow bending, forearm going up .. focusing .. concentrating .. drifting and floating .. floating and drifting .. seeing the top of a staircase .. going deeper .. and deeper .. noting the Circular staircase .. moving down ..deeper.. ..now very deep, to its Center ... "

" I'D LIKE TO SPEAK WITH THE INNERMOST.. "

Suddenly and unexpectedly, Robert's eyes popped *open!* [22] ..
Remaining fixed .. straight ahead .. *Eyes Wide~Open!* .. arm up
the gaze convergent .. everything motionless .. immovable ..

The small office felt as if filled with boundless awareness; it
was palpable, dense like a force, awesome or overwhelming .. [23] ?

The Voice was slow. Deliberate. Unhurried and ineffable.
My questions quietly put, its responses were straightforward.

" *WHO ARE YOU?* "

I am g ..

My thoughts moved into higher gear.

"G-d? ... is that what is about to be said? "

*All the time I'd seen Robert, invariably there was balance, nothing at
all off the deep end .. Continuing to myself in split-second, Could this
voice sense what outer Robert might be ~ and I am now ~ thinking and
feeling, "Might this be too much to handle?"*

... Its cadence tranquil, serene ... it continued ...

I don't really want to say, I am God.
I don't know how it will be taken .. but I am ..
an inner spiritual guide ...
I am ... God~like.
I preserve ~him.

---

[22] *In my experience subjects' eyes had always remained closed.*   *11-23-2008*

[23] *Was the energy imagined? Indeed it felt real, surpassing my conscious
expectations of the time.*   *5-22-2005*

It responded further and described a basic function,

*I feel things, when they are right or
when they are not right.*

This one-sentence response hit home, its function cracking an enigma persisting throughout therapy. It provided precisely what Robert sought for fourteen months.

All questions asked in behalf of Robert were answered. Like a laser, super-computer of the mind, it honed in on mysteries, themes and nuances of childhood and adulthood.

It possessed tremendous awareness and surgical precision. Before stopping, a general question was posed,

" *Is there more you would you like to say to Robert?* "

Yes

I love him.
One Voice.   One Person.
The Deep and Real.
TRUST ME.

~

Words from Robert's core, germane to questions stated and unstated: poignant, clear, concentrated, capturing both sides of a dialectic paradox, "Is it me or is it not me?"

The fascinating conclusion was a declaration of trust!...how or who and what to trust.

As Robert was brought back up from the hypnosis, I suggested *"only with your permission"* a connection or integration between outer Robert and his core *"occurring at the count of four."* [24]

0 .. 1 .. 2 .. 3 .. **4** .. 5 .. 6 .. 7 .. 8

Right as he came out of trance Robert disclosed,

" I wish I could have said, Yes ~ to the connection."

He reported at 0-1-2-3,

"Really was dazed, things crushing in on me.
Or me, crushing out on things."

At 4 to 8 he was,

"Breathing better...came out less dazed than
I thought."

Robert explained,

"I had access to a deeper level ... More Honesty.

It was like an <u>avenue</u> coming out of my <u>heart</u>."

The experience was transformational. Obscure no more were his concerns about trust, integration, self-sufficiency. These areas had been unraveled and deciphered. To Robert this Voice was his inner compass, *"Always there, if one listens for it."*

We journeyed into this inquiry with two sets of perceptions, his and mine. We found a new outlook and ideas previously hidden. This was a fresh, refined and highly focussed thought process, not available before to him nor to me until now.

---

[24] *Not knowing then if integration was a reasonable goal or not, I approached this with reservation and caution. The description, "One Voice, One Person," lead me to consider such a connection yet thus far it seems there may exist also, an inherent separation.*   -edit. 3-8-2005

As a therapist committed to objectivity, I deliberated, how shall this wondrous phenomenon be taken? It surely provided superb, precise, clear and precious, answers and responses. This was astonishing to say the least, yet attempting to remain clinically neutral I questioned, "How for real is this?" [25]

My professional training related to a "judicious use of self." The interpersonal process helps to gauge what is taking place. The therapist's own person can supply pertinent information and an overall perspective.

As facilitator it was imperative to maintain equivocation, even though I had witnessed an intense psychological power, clarity and wisdom.

"G- ?" Robert did not recall it this way--he remembered only an "inner spiritual Guide." Robert was conventional, and not invested in ecclesiastic thought, that I knew about. In the first fourteen months of therapy, neither religious nor spiritual matters had been discussed.

My basic concern was, how will Robert respond to this high-power development? How would he take all this: will it be positive for him? Might there be any adverse effects?

Robert, as the person and professional editor he was, maintained equanimity, and seemed to incur no difficulty at all. To him, this significant experience felt completely natural.

It was organic; and how hypnotherapy went.

---

[25] *Analogously, a research hypnosis organization tracked veracity of past-life regressions. Outside proof was not found, however, clinical researchers did conclude the regressions often were worthwhile for individuals.*   *5-21-2005*

Previously unknown to Robert, this inner Voice was instantly perceived as a natural phenomenon and a part of his life.

Robert emerged from trance with an unequivocal clarification of what he called an age-old question of religion.

He wondered no more about spirituality.

Now he knew.

❖

How could I convey what had just happened here?

If only I had taped this! Or maybe it wasn't meant to be that way. Since it felt as if I had just been conversing with the Burning Bush, how much of this could have been captured on audiotape anyway?

I decided, from here on out it would be prudent or obligatory to tape record the Inner core sessions. The decision was fortunate.

Next time we have a transcript.

~

The volcano

Whatever it is you want
~ they're there.

<4>

Joseph

Winds of Light

May 11th, 1989

I'm not out to harm anybody

I'm only here to h~e~l~p.

Just relax and l.o.o.k.

And it'll be there.

Name	Age	Occupation	Inner contact	Prior therapy
Joe	42	Teacher	5-11-89	10 months

You know what the inner core looks like - at first?
[Ah, ha, ha, ha, ha . . .]
It was green..because it's all ideas.
I see the green first and then the thought comes in.
And then, umm...it was.. um..just..there was a light..
just a light.
And then like..Winds of light just..going around.
And in those winds of light is anything you want.
Whatever it is you want ~ they're there.

Then I tried to figure, where is it in my body?
It's, it's like it's all around.

- Joe

*J*oseph was a virtuoso; an unusual person with a clear goal,
"*Peace at all times!*"

His motive for therapy was self-actualization. Joseph explained he wanted *"peace all of the time ... kind of like a Jesus or Buddha or Moses."*

My first thought was, "Let's be real here." (.. nine months prior to the emergence of the Inner core).[26] Even with stress reduction, hypnosis, biofeedback and all the other therapies, how would I ever assist him to do *that?* Yet this was his goal.

His aims were lofty, and overly so I thought, if Joe meant this literally. I gently countered, "Do you think even Jesus, Buddha and Moses had some stress in their lives?"

Fifteen years of meditation had kept Joe's stress to a minimum.

A decade earlier, he had resolved his long-standing depression through three years of therapy. Thus he was no longer depressed, as he had been "for years and years as a kid."

Joe explained, "Therapy helped a lot but didn't go far enough. It never got to the real culprit, the ego. I want to replace the ego with the true self."

In sync with Joe's aims and thoughts in general, still I wondered, where could he and we go from here?

Peace at *all* times...in this world in which we live?

---

[26] *I am fascinated reading this two and a half-years later, comparing my reactions now to then. I wondered if I could be of any help at all. Peace at all times. My reaction was, "impossible." People basically needed, I had thought, to resolve traumas, to deal with stressors, and expect the latter inevitably as a part of life.*　　　*1-14-1991*

A Virtuoso.

Joe happened to possess a tremendous ability in imagery. These talents had not been appreciated by him; and he was not encouraged by anyone while growing up nor as an adult.

At the beginning[27] we determined he had high to excellent hypno-abilities, and that he was particularly tuned into visual imagery. "Pictures" generously sprang to his mind.

Three weeks later *"The Three Screens"* were described to Joe. Already having confidence in his abilities, I mentioned to him, *"You'll be able to do this yourself."* [28]

Joe was easily able to visualize these three screens--without hypnosis. It wasn't necessary to facilitate any trance because he could see an image whenever encouraged. In a brief time, this ability became available to him whenever he wished.

Homeopathic Hypnosis.

Only one time over the year was a formal hypnosis utilized, and that was, "FIXING THE SEAL." [29]

Six weeks later (only his *second* formal hypnosis), this time it was attempting to reach an Inner core.

Or was this a *de*-hypnosis, to find the true Self?

---

[27] *At the very first session July 6, 1988 for some reason we performed the* HIP (Hypnotic Induction Profile) *which showed high hypno-abilities with a possible slight ambivalence? "My arm was heavy, like cement...it didn't want to (lift up) but the balloon was stronger - and up it went."* 10-9-2008

[28] *I had not said it before this way, but for some reason did here.* "

[29] *On March 30, 1989. The process is described elsewhere.* "

Self-actualization.

Joe had overcome depression. He didn't appear depressed at all, certainly not with me. From the beginning a sense of joy permeated the atmosphere of our working together.

His approach was genuine; and he was a teacher. I could easily see students enjoying his classes.

We had discussed perfectionism, and revising his expectations, accepting inevitable aspects of life. I appreciated what Joe meant by concern over Ego--with a caveat: ego is necessary to be able to function. [30]

Joe didn't disagree with those ideas yet still maintained his goal for his ego: to dissolve it & to replace it. Despite my qualms about quixotic goals, I did not see Joe's ideas as harmful to him. It would be up to Joe if we were to proceed. We agreed to work together in therapeutic exploration, which we did for nine months before any formal hypnosis.

Joe's imaging ability was a natural gift he always had but it had been unappreciated, disparaged and diminished by others. This gift was appreciated and nurtured by me, and later by Joe. He utilized it first in the office, then often outside on his own.

His use of imagery became paramount. Whenever he wanted or needed to know anything, I reminded him to simply check, what is the image. He'd momentarily pause, look within, smile, and say, "Ahh, this is what I see."

The image was invariably there.

---

[30] *Having assumed Joe moved far beyond our first meeting, I had not thought much about his initially stated goals, until rereading my notes a couple of years later.*   *-1990s*
  Regarding ego, it depends on which aspects are in operation.
  This is discussed in general terms in Part Three.   *7-25-2010*

Joe had achieved much of the growth he'd been looking for and although not in a personal relationship, he was comfortable with himself and his life.

Ten months after beginning therapy, I shared with Joe, there is something I've been working on, about which he too might have an interest, and that is, "getting to the Inner Core!"

Joe immediately indicated a desire to try this, and before we continued, I received his permission to begin audio taping.

Thoughts flashed through my mind: *"This is all new terrain, but not to forget: I know my craft, the hypnosis is well honed; and I know Joe, his psychodynamics and hypnotic profile..."*

I'm aware of Joe's excitement anxiety. As taping begins, he switches gears slightly; I attend to and help to counterbalance. We maneuver around an underlying tension of expectancy...as preview imagery about the Inner core begins to bubble up.

Our aims now intentional, the hypnotic process is becoming operational; the outcome is not fully predictable.

~

Joe and the Volcano.

TRANSCRIPT   *May 11, 1989*

KEY: *CB*=CB   J=Joe   **Bold**=Inner core

~

CB: .. *[turning on tape equipment]* ... but before you..--

J: ..and what?..you're going to tell me why we're going for..huh?

CB: tell you what?-

J: -why were going to..for?-

CB: why?-

CB: Actually I was just gonna get into..it. I was going to
ask you to tell *me,* *(little laugh)* what you'd like me
to accomplish, if any, y'kno in terms of, if you have
any..statements, questions, um, it's really-

J: I-   *CB:* My, it's really-   *J:* Well-

CB: -it's *your* relationsh-

J: -the *other* thing is..I've never *been* to the core..I don't know
what it is actually..I want to see what it is but I think that..
if you get to your core..and you're real..um..aware of WHERE
it is or WHAT it is, uahm... *(probably an image - an answer:)* it
allows you, just to function at a much higher level. It-i-it-ita
has to do with energy. You don't have to expend, for myself
anyway, expend great amounts of energy with *worry* and all
kinds of *craziness,* worrying about this or, *fighting* with this
or that, and I think the core will give you the answers, on
not to..*waste* that energy.

CB: The core gets right, right to (the essential)-..That's what
you like-

J: Yea, right..Cause y'kno' I mean, --in my life I feel like I
have a million and one things that I still want to do,
/CB: yeah./ -and I can't horse around anymore with
wasting my energy, y'kno', worrying about this
and worrying about that. I just want to get
my stuff *done* that I want to do!

CB: Well, of all people that I work with, you, do have an, an
indirect access to that core.

J: great.

CB: -It's almost direct, in terms of the images you asked for.

J: um hmm.

CB: -You ask for the answer, and you get the answer.. through
the image.

J: ok, yeah.

C: -so you already have a..a pipeline.. */J: yeah../*
-At least I think that's coming from the core--isn't it?-,
   /J: yeah../   -or..where's it come from?

J: -See, when you say "core", you know what I see?
   /C: hym.? / -It's a *circle*...like that.. */C: yah./*
   -That's what I see...Earlier I saw it as blue.

                                        (4 seconds)

   Now why am I seeing *lava* in there? I don't know.
      Why am I seeing lava...

                                        (excitedly..)

C: What's lava?- *(Mutual laughter!)* -a *Volcano*..!

J: *(laughing)* oh, -I know why it's core-...I know why it's
   core.. Oh I see what I'm seeing...We're talking about a
   core.. we're talking about a *core of the earth*..and in a
   sense we're talking about, what does Jung call it?..this,
   this consciousness?

C: *Collective.*

J: -*collective consciousness* type of thing. So the core is
   kind of...-I see what I'm doing-...it's like a collective
   consciousness, and the core is where -oh we were talking
   about these mystical stuff and all that stuff?- that's what
   that *is!*

It's a subcon- it's your subconsciousness that knows everything - just because it *knows*. Where it got the information?
   I don't know where it got it but it knows. */C: um/*
      -That's what, that's what the core is...for me.

C: Well, going in on that base, why don't we- why don't
   we start? But is there any question or comments you
   want me to..ah..*(quietly put)* convey for you, to the core?

                                        3 second pause

48

J: (- quietly) What do you mean?

C: -how- */J:* -well-

    CB and *J:* " *[Talking at the same time...Loudly]* "

J: -you know what?-

C: well- [31]

J: I just want to tell you, it's kind of a little scary, but it's ok.
I'm.. It's.. If I'm scared a little bit, that means, *oooh I'm
about to discover something.* Ahmm!- *(deep, guttural laughter)*
Ahmm..just that I get maximum use of that core, I want
to be able to use it effectively, and really go with it!

C: okay.

*J: (Again, looking at an image...) Oh I see why it's bubbling,
and it's bubbling because it has a lot of things it wants to
accomplish.*

    It wants to burst out and do all this stuff. */C:* ok.[32]

      ~

C: OK, well why don't we get started on ... *(the hypnosis)*
    ...the footstool...

    {Getting set, positioning the footstool}

J: (laughingly, nervously?) Yes, I was going to say f -stool,
the STOOL, STOOL.

C: (Couldn't hear the word) Oh.. the FOOTstool?!, footstool.

J: yes.

C: I didn't *think* you were referring to stool.[33]

---

[31] *I knew it too.*

[32] This description stuck with me through the rest of 1989 and thereafter.
    " *It's bubbling because it has a lot of things it wants to accomplish.
It wants to burst out and do all this stuff.* "

[33] *..some tension relief.*

J: no, no, I started to think in my mind, am I going to sit on it? or what? *(some laughing)*

C: Remember *that?* *(The footstool)*

J: Yeah, now I remember. - [34]

Going into Hypnosis.   *{hypnotic induction}*

J: (breathing out with relief) aohhh.

C: Ok, getting comfortable, with feet up...hands resting comfortably, either as they are, on your lap, or on the arm of the couch..

J: just like, how bout just like this?...

C: oh, ok.

J: fine.

C: ok. ...and then, start with...looking forward, looking at me here, -and then on the count of one, doing one thing, on the count of two, doing two things..and three, three things. One, looking up, to the top of your eyebrows - eyes closing . . .   {ETC.}

(Forearm floating up)   *{going deep}*

OK, going deeper and deeper...going down that stairway, perhaps a purple stairway *(his prior color)*,...and it can be, if you wish, it can be a circular stairway..down that circular stairway...down to the center...of the circle.. ..the goal...when we get down...to the center... we'll be reaching the core...

Counting yourself down... 8 down to one down to 0...

---

[34] *The focus had been Joe's natural imagery without formal hypnosis, and thus without a footstool. This time the procedure is hypnosis; as we did ten months earlier, we utilize a footrest.*   *3-23-2005*

8 - 7 - 6 *(Relaxing, soothing, checking level of trance)* - 5 -
4 - 3 - 2 - 1 - and 0. *And I'd like to talk to the Inner...*
Let me know..when you're there..when you're ready..

I'D LIKE TO TALK TO THE INNER ... HELLO!

A Guttural Sound   " **YA~** "

with a Nod

8 seconds

DO YOU HAVE A NAME? ...

It is COMPLETELY QUIET
~A Deep, Melodious voice emerges

8 seconds

I am called Life.

..OK.. HOW OLD ARE YOU?

6 seconds

I am over a hundred years old.

..OK.. HOW LONG HAVE YOU BEEN, BEEN HERE WITH JOE?

2 seconds

I've been here forever.

..IS HE AWARE OF YOU?

Yes.

AND YOU'RE AWARE OF HIM?

Yes.   *(Outside sound)*

..DOES HE COMMUNICATE WITH YOU, DIRECTLY?

2-3 seconds

Sometimes, but mostly indirectly

..OK.. ARE YOU...?- **he's-** *-AH..*

..he's afraid of me.

..OH... WHAT'S HE AFRAID OF?

3-4 seconds

He's afraid of being overpowered by me.

..SHOULD HE BE AFRAID? [35]

No, not at all.

(V-e-r-y gently)

..K.. WHY NOT?..

I'm not out to harm anybody.
I'm only here to h~e~l~p. [36]

..IS HE AFRAID OF YOUR POWER?

Yeah, afraid of the power and af.ah.afraid because he doesn'..he doesn't underst.a..nd.

WELL HE SAYS HE'D LIKE TO MAKE MAXIMUM USE, AH,
USE YOU EFFECTIVELY..REALLY GO WITH IT.
..YOU'RE AWARE THAT HE IS-HE IS AFRAID..

Hm hmm.

..DO YOU HAVE ANY, UM, SUGGESTIONS FOR HIM?

He has to come and look what this is. He's got to see what, what I am, what the core is, what I am.

.OK.

---

[35] *My own thought at the time, "..and should I be?"*   *3-23-2005*

[36] *Much later I realized Joe had full amnesia about these statements on fear even though he alluded to it earlier. As open as Joe was to imagery, his unacknowledged fear was behind avoidance of the deeper inner self. Ultimately we went over this part of the tape--much to Joe's surprise.*
4-22-1991

HOW CAN HE COME AND LOOK?

He just has to look.

AND THERE~THERE YOU ARE.

Hm hmm.

.OK.. SO IT'S THAT SIMPLE.

Yes.

OK.

7 seconds

..ANY OTHER IDEAS FOR HIM, WHY HE'S NOT LOOKING?
... HOW HE CAN TUNE INTO YOU, SOME MORE?...

W'll all he has to do is just ~ relax...and l o o k.
All he has to do is relax and l o o k . . .
And it'll be there.

..OK... IS THERE ANYTHING THAT HE..HE NEEDS TO KNOW, THAT
HE, AH, THAT HE DOESN'T KNOW, ABOUT YOU, BECAUSE HE'S..
HE HAS A NUMBER OF QUESTIONS.. **Yah-**

First of all, he has to, eh..
He needs to know that I c a r e.
I'm here to h e l p.
I mean absolutely no harm.
And, he doesn't have to be afraid at a~ l~ l.

NOT AT ALL ~   *(I'm being soothed here too.)*

Not at all, and that I in fact do exist.

HE NEEDS TO KNOW THAT.. **Hm hmm.**

..AND TO TRUST..   **Yes.**

THERE ARE TIMES THAT HE DOESN'T, DOESN'T KNOW THAT?

Yah. that's right.

HE DOESN'T TRUST THAT.

Doesn't trust.

4 seconds

..BUT YOU'RE THERE.

All the time.

7 seconds

...UH, ONE, ONE OF THE QUESTIONS HE MAY HAVE..UHHH.. CONCERNS .. OR ISSUES IN HIS LIFE ...

HE TALKS ABOUT CARRYING AROUND A LOT OF BURDEN AT TIMES, AND A LOT OF.. hym hymm.. *..HURT, AND PRESSURE ... FROM PARENTS.*

DO YOU HAVE ANY THOUGHTS ON HIS..PARENTS?...FEELINGS?

W.. I think he needs to -let me look at this-
He needs to look at them as human beings,
without a connection to him.
..And he'll get those answers if he looks
into that core and sees that.

..THEIR CORE? [37]

N- a-a-my- me! as the core.   *OH.*
The answers are there.

IF-

And he needs to cut off, that ribbon
or that cord that puts, that binds them together.

---

[37] *Mostly checking perspective.*

...HE NEEDS TO CUT OFF THAT RIBBON...[38]

Hym hymm.

5 seconds

...AND WHEN HE DOES THAT, WHAT WILL HE ACHIEVE?

**When he cuts off the ribbon, he no longer has to act.
He then sees them as human beings,....and is able
to look from an, from a, from an objective point
of view..instead of a subjective point of view.**

**He also, then, can get on with his own life.
And do what <u>he</u> wants to do.**

**And take what he wants from the parent.
And discard what he wants,
And do what <u>he</u> wants to do.**

*SO CUTTING THE RIBBON DOESN'T MEAN HE, HE STILL
..CAN'T T<u>A</u>KE.*

Not at all, no, no ... no.

**He's also afraid that if he cuts the ribbon, the
parents will go away and he won't have a parent,
but that's not the case ...**

That's not what's gonna happen.

... they'll always be there.

*IS IT A, IS IT A DIFFERENT CONNECTION WHEN
HE CUTS THE RIBBON, OR- /?*

**Well then the connec- then the connection is one of,
of just liking each other. That's the connection.**

---

[38] *I remember my initial reservation, surprise, and then appreciating
the artistry here ... I hadn't ever heard it put this way before.*   *3-23-05*

*The connections, they come and they go and they
... do what they want. That doesn't mean that
they go away forever. That doesn't mean
that they float away.*

..JUST MEANS THEY'RE DIFFERENT.

A different rela..a different relationship.
..OK..

10 seconds

..I- I'M WONDERING IF..AH..WHO IS TH- WHO
SUPPLIES THE IMAGES..TO JOE?

I do.

OK..SO WHEN HE ASKS YOU, YOU COME RIGHT UP WITH THE...
Hm hmm.   ...IMAGES.   *Yes.*
..SO HE HE HAS THAT..THAT WAY OF COMMUNICATING
WITH YOU-

*~ So what he does is he taps, and it's like the..he
bounces to me, and then from me, I.. the
image is bounced off.*

And he sees the image.

*But he doesn't need to..bounce the image;
he just has to look right in me.*

SO HE DOESN'T NEE-, HE DOESN'T NEED THE IMAGE.

Well what he, what he...   -IF HE LOOKS RIGHT IN-

*Well-..he..he, see, what he does is he, he says,
"...ok give me the image..."*

56

It's like a ray of light bounces to me, and I
bounce the image on, on wherever, on a screen
or whatever, and he sees that image.

He doesn't need to do that.

Because, all he sees is the Image.

But if he comes and looks right at Me, I will
give him not only the image; I will give him
the feeling that goes with it.

OHH, OK... [39]

And the words and the thoughts.
It's, it's a more complete-

-COMPLETE-

-com-, it's more complete if he looks at me,
than if he just looks at that image.

NOW DOES HE KNOW HOW TO LOOK DIRECTLY AT YOU?

Yeah sure he does. . but he's afraid.

OH.

And he's afraid of the feeling part; it's much easier
to deal with the picture, and then let the feeling in
little by little by little.

But he's afraid to look at me directly, because then
he's going to get the feeling.

And the feeling will hurt, and he's afraid of that,
he doesn't want to look at hurt.

---

[39] *Yes! ~ an Ah-ha surprise, so clear and simple. This made sense
as to an underlying subtlety in Joe's concern, heretofore unstated.*

YOU'RE KIND OF SAYING THAT HURT'S O.K...

Well, what I'm saying is,

eh..y/kno ..there was a pl- a time when he couldn't deal with the hurt.

But he can deal with that feeling, or he knows how to deal with that now. So he doesn't need to deal only with pictures.

He can deal with the <u>whole</u> <u>thing</u>.

OKAY ..I HAVE A QUESTION ABOUT..HIM AN-AND HIS RELATION-SHIPS.., AND HOW...WHAT'S BEST FOR HIM.

A'hem.

-MUMM, WHAT DO YOU THINK?

Well. I think that he's, uh, he encloses himself and hides away. He needs to get out and, meet new people, be out with different kinds of people.

He limits himself, too much. Again it has to do with feelings, of being hurt by those feelings.

But he knows how to deal with that.

He doesn't have to be afraid.

HOW MUCH DOES THIS IS RELATED TO- TO HIS CONCERNS ABOUT PEOPLE?

Well they're re-, they're, certainly they're related to that; um, but they're also related to his family, and how they've made him feel bad.

And umm, so it's kind of mixed in there; it's mixed together.

. . .

OK... CAN HE GET BACK TO YOU, OR DEAL WITH YOU
ABOUT ANY QUESTIONS?

S~u~r~e. Anytime.

OK..ANY QUESTIONS ABOUT- ..ANYTHING?

About Anything.

5 seconds

DO YOU FEEL FREE TO COME OUT IN HIS LIFE? ..FEEL FREE
TO COME OUT..   **No.**

**Not always because if I come out at certain times
it becomes frightening for him.**

**And so I don't have permission to do that
all the time.**

SO YOU, YOU NEED PERMISSION.

Oh yes.
FROM-... / **Yeah** */ -FROM HIM?* **Yeah.**

He has to come looking for me.

**I will help, but I can't just
...dominate the whole thing.**

He has to ask me for that help.

Or has to look in me for the answers.

WOULD THERE BE TIMES THAT YOU COULD COME OUT, LET'S
SAY TO CONNECT WITH ANOTHER PERSON...IN HIS LIFE? [40]

I don't understand.

---

[40] *This question as asked felt fuzzy to me. ... "How would one's inner core
connect with another person, or with the other's Core...?" Response to this
question felt well-tuned to my feelings as I asked it.*   3-25-2005

UMM.. IN LET'S SAY A RELATIONSHIP WITH ANOTHER PERSON. COULD HE AND YOU COME OUT TOGETHER?

Sure.

~ you mean, without, permission?

WELL, IN A NATURAL...FASHION?

Sure, yeah I could see that happening; sure.

WHEN IT'S OKAY, KIND OF NATURAL-

When it's okay, and also when I know it's not going to be something threatening.

OK.. SO THAT WOULD BE OKAY WITH HIM?

Hm hmm, yes.

AND WITH YOU?

And with me.

SO..OK...IS THERE ANYTHING THAT YOU WANT ME TO CONVEY, BACK TO HIM? THAT YOU HAVEN'T ALREADY?

N-, well, he knows this, but... [41]

He has permission to look in here any time he wants. The answers are all here. And, umm, I'm here to help ~ I'm not here to hurt or whatever ~ I'm here to help.

..OK..

6 seconds

WELL THANK YOU FOR TALKING WITH ME.

Emhm, you're welcome.

---

[41] *Joe already knows this...Response was partly for me, my concerns. Without saying so, I did want to hear it again myself.   3-25-05*

WOULD IT BE OK TO TALK AGAIN?

S U R E ,, Anytime.   *A highly Cooperative*
                                         Deep melodious tone

OKAY. OK. THANK YOU.

~

Now just, drifting off..Relaxing...and connecting in any way... that would be useful and helpful..that you'd like... connected to the other in some way -or in many ways-...now just drifting...flowing... being wherever you'd like to be..

And finding that staircase..that circular staircase..anyplace on that..going from 0 to 1 place..by the time you get to 8, you'll feel refreshed.. relaxed.. together.. feeling fine.. energized. bringing back all of this .. or as much of this as you wish., this experience.

Now going from 0 to 1..and to 2.. going up, and around that circular staircase..3..and to 4 - 5 - 6 - 7 - and 8. On 3, with your eyes closed, getting ready..2, rolling up your eyes, making a fist with the hand that's up..and 1, letting your eyes come in to focus, and the hand float down.

~

CB: *And--How are you feeling?*

J: *(a little laugh!)   F-i-n-e. I love that. That was g-r-e-a-t... That was g-r-e-a-t...!*

J: You know what the Inner Core looks like-? /CB: umm?/
        - at first?

Ah, ha, ha, ha, ha- *It was green..because it's all ideas.* [42]
I see the green first and then the thought comes in.

---

[42] *Winds of Light: see Inner work 4-17-90 with my friend Kenneth Ingram Goldman, six months five days before he passed on 22 Oct. 1990. 4-22-91*

And then, umm...it was.. um..just...there was a Light..
  just a Light.

And then like...Winds of light just...going around.

And in those winds of light is anything you want.

Whatever it is you want ~ they're there.

J: *(to himself)* ..and uh, what else...?

Then I tried to figure, *where is it in my body?* It's, it's
  like it's all around.

C: I didn't ask that; I could have.[43]

J: *It's like right in here.* *(excitedly)* No, I know-I know-
  I know. I saw it; I mean it was right there.
  I saw it. *(making gestures)*

C: Yes, these two? shoulders? around the body?

J: Yeah

C: -or in the body?

J: Yeah, yeah, well, *it's not _IN_ the body.*

  It's like superimposed _ON_ the body.

CB: Yah.

J: *It's like a big circle, and it's everywhere.*

C: yeah, ummm. It's below your head?

J: Yeah, but I think..if I look at it here..that's what I saw
  now. But it could shift.

J: *It could become real small, or it could be expanded..*

CB: That's certainly different than the western idea of being
  in the head. It's right there in the whole body */J: yeah/*
  -and it can shift.   / *J: Yeah.*

CB: Well what do you think about som- ?
  Did you hear *every*thing?

---

[43] *I had thought about asking just that but hadn't.*

J: *Oh sure!*

CB: Okay, in terms of, you don't _have_ to-   /   *J:*   *(laughing)*

CB: -to use the images.

J: Right! It's those *feelings*-

CB: You can go direct.

J: Yeah but it's- -Absolutely! It's those fuckin' feelings!

C: *(laughing)*

J: -like when I saw the image of my mom? -immediately
I cut off. I didn't want to feel what I felt at the time.

C :   *Yeah.*

J: I didn't want to..aaagggh..you know? *[my laughing]* -
..aaagggh..you know? I don't want to do that.

...But it's OK to do it, because it gets, if it gets it out in
the open into the light, and then it can, you can get rid
of it. Or deal with it, or whatever you're going to do
with it, bury it or whatever you want to do with it,
or send it out to outer space.

CB: Or even heal it.

J: Or, yeah, or heal it or whatever you want to do with it.

C: yeah..

J: *Wow!*...

CB: Well.. *(Mutual laughter)* ..we did it.

J: Well we're late; we're running late here. *(laughing)*

CB: Just on time.

J: Wow, just on time, wow. Wooo, I'm going to have to
play with this all week long... Yeah, I saw, I see what
I'm going to use it tomorrow for, ha-ha-h
Let me borrow your pen. *(writing checque)* ..that's to
the Family *Stress* Clinic?

C: Yes...remember that word? [44]

J: That was good. I *loved* that!

J: You oughta do that with everybody! Really! That was- that was-

See now, immediately I focussed on something: I don't like to be in front of crowds and stuff? So tomorrow I have a -what-do-you-call-it- we have an assembly. Now..as I'm doing it I'll just go right in there and not feel fearful or *whatever* ~ The answer's right there!

CB: Oh yeah. Yeah.

J: Date is what? *(finishing checque)* -the eleventh...

C: I'd like to do it with *me*. *(laughter)*

J: You oughta do it! Seriously, get somebody to do it for you.. *W-o-w.*

CB: I'll have to..have to work with them on it.

J: Yeah!

C: I've done some of that, but that's exactly right: that the answer is always ... is right there.

J: Now I've- you kno' I have said that-!!, for YEARS-!- I've said that!

CB: -but the way you just said it-

J: Yeah! But it's a-, but *it's a different thing*-! You know what I mean?- *it's a different thing!*

~

CB: So two weeks?

J: Yeah... *(set time)* .. Let's see what I do with that... All right, we'll see you, *LATER !!*

---

[44] *He was exceedingly* un*stressed.*

64

This was a peak experience.

An inner awareness clarified itself, and Joe's inner and outer worlds, precisely. A radical explanation of adult family dynamics was revelatory. With beauty and artistry, it effortlessly brought this all forth.

In explaining how imagery is communicated beginning with the request to, and response back from the Inner core, it pinpointed a previously unknown process, and a hidden fear related to it.

When Joe came out of the hypnosis he was ecstatic. He thought he remembered it all, although later I realized he had missed parts. As pleased as he was, and I as well, still we needed to follow Joe's responses with care.

Thankfully this time, all of it was taped.

~

With three of four adults,[45] an apparent inner consciousness had clearly provided self-description and psychological/social analysis. The three were consistent, and in each case the Inner's statements seemed remarkably correct. I had known all four patients well, three over a long period of time, yet here were fresh surprising new insights and concepts.

I could resonate with and admire their ingenuity and accuracy. In my judgment no patient nor therapist had such analytic and integrative ability--with ease and precision--as did these.

Now, would this hold up with others?

---

[45] *Not realizing, the fourth as well had provided its form of data.*

The Second Wave

"For it is exceedingly close to you,

in your mouth and in your heart.."

The Second Wave

Discovery

Here

I feel good that- I- have the-
　　　　have the inner feeling, to me.

<5>

Jonathan

May 19th, 1989

A Hole in One

Name	Age	Occupation	Inner contact	Prior therapy
Jonathan	15	Student	5-19-89	2 yrs 3 mon
			6-21-89	

Does he check with you, very often?

" *N-o-o.* "

Does he know about you?

" *I think so.* "

What do you take care of?

"*All the..inner..thoughts.*"

*J*onathan mostly didn't say much.
His responses were, *"Yeah"* or *"No"*
or when pressed, *"I have, no idea."*

Jonathan was a quiet and gentle youngster, twelve when we began and fifteen years old when we met the Inner core--this makes him the youngest of the pioneers to reach it. [46]

Jon and his little sister lived in two domiciles, staying with their mother on weekdays and their dad on weekends.

Jonathan's mother was a take-it-slow, feel it through, be careful, act-very-deliberately kind of person. His dad was action--oriented, do it right now, and forget-any-funny-stuff. Each parent was fully committed to his or her own approach, wishing the same qualities for his or her children.

Trying to comply or adapt to possibly polar opposite styles was a challenge. He and his family had suffered a long series of losses. A year prior to beginning therapy, Jonathan's school determined a "significant learning disability," and Jon was placed in programs he did not particularly like.

Therapy moved along gradually, and with time a subtle but solid therapeutic alliance developed with Jonathan. Over the years Jon's verbalizations remained minimalistic and circumscribed; typically, *"Yeah."* ... *"No."* ... *"I have, no idea."*

Jonathan stuttered since early age; although this concerned him he did not really want to talk about it, until in therapy Jon had begun to consider hypnotherapy. Based on the HIP (Hypnotic Induction Profile), we became aware he might have significantly high hypno-ability.

---

[46] *... until his younger sister briefly, six months later.*

Permission was provided for utilizing hypnosis, to include emerging work with inner core, if and when the time was right for Jonathan, and if he was interested.

The time became right on *May 19*. Jon came to his session with a very big crisis, one he *really* wanted help with!

He was to present his *first* speech,[47] and *"not only* to the class--but also to the *whole school*...including *all the parents!"* "What," I wondered to myself, "is going on with this; isn't the school overdoing something here?"

Jon was not seeking a way out, such as assisting vis-à-vis his school. Jon's own plan was hypnosis and self-hypnosis, and now, his public presentation was approaching oh so shortly. He wanted to get to basics.

As we start hypnotherapy the first time, I ask Jon about the possibility of making contact with the Inner. Any reservations on *my* part are counter-mandated by the readiness, motivation and critically strong need on *his* part.

May 19, 1989

J=Jonathan   C=Cliff

C: ...you know, what you think about it, and what you hope to get from it..you know, from..from the hypnosis. ..Any ideas?

J: Nnnn-not..not right now.

C: .ok..umm..

J: Probably to..umm..not stutter anymore.

C: 'k.. (5 sec)

---

[47] *Nearly all people are fearful of public speaking.*

C: ..So, we'll see what kind of ah..effect..you know..it has. It might..clear up a lot. It might get- /*J:* yeah./ -the ball rolling ..there's a whole ..you know.. it might start something..continue some things that you're already working on.. something we'll see.. *(quietly)* how it works.. Yr..er what are your ideas about stuttering?

J: Iit-It's prob-ably something that comes and goes.

C: oh. Do you know when it comes and when it goes?

J: N-no.

C: Uumm..y' know I've-I've said before I've noticed that when you're father's sitting next to you it's different than when it's just you and me. So..does th't-have-anything- /*J:* sortof-/ -do with it? Have you noticed a difference. Or, not?

J: Nn-no.

C: oh, ok..ahh- So. Ok, so we'll work on that.. (doing hypnosis with the stuttering). Any-any thoughts on that other thing I was talking about, talking to the Inside?

J: emmm..nno.

C: That sounds more..umm..it sounds to me like you have a different feeling about that one- /*J:* yeah./ -right now.

C: *(breathing in).* Ummm..can you say what?

J: Umm..prob-ab-ly to..like- get- the- sstuttering under control, then- go on -to ss- on- and then go on- to talking with the Inside. /*T:*ok./ Or I- or I could do it (what's) talking to the Inside first, and then do the stuttering.

C:..Yeah. .Or a combination thereof. *(?)*

J: yeah.

C: ..Well we can see what works best, n'how it works out for you- /*J: yeah.* / -an' I noticed when you were kinda looking at the microphone an'- getting more energy, you're stuttering less!-

J: yeah.

C: -you notice that?

J: umm, a little..

C: -well- it-jus'-seems-like-a- more of a flow..

J: yeah.

C: ..So maybe when you give that speech, that'll be the same.. energy of kind of..helping with that flow. ..Well we'll see..how- how it all works.   *(a possibility, a wakeful idea, an observation of Jon)*

(Creaky chair, moving)

C: Well, we'll start with ah... Well in terms of the, y'kno', what to do first, whether to, work on the stuttering or work on talking with the Inside, do you have any, any f- any feelings about that?

J: No-o. *(with a yawn)*

C: Either one..(?)

J: *(post-yawn)* Either one's fine with me.

C: Ok...umm...Ok, well-let's a- start with- getting y'kno the relax.. ation..and um going into ah place-

J: yeah.   *(more creaky chair, getting positioned, pillows for arm)*

C: -Let's see.. And umm.. I'll get that stool, here.. Did we do it on this side before, /J: I-/ -over here?   *(Selecting an arm)*

J: -I think so.

C: Yeah! I think that's the- ok.

{Getting set}

C: ... ok, (we'll) start with getting as comfortable..as possible..arms resting..resting on..pillows and-

J: uh huh

76

C: (-) -Ok, and then at ONE..ok..(looking) up..towards the top of your eyebrows, and towards the top of your head, holding your eyes up..TWO, letting th' eyelids come down - the eyes up (to top)..ta- taking a deep breath..holding it..n' then THREE, letting the eyes RELAX and the breathing b'comes easier and easier, and the body floats, and one hand or the other, probably the right hand, floats UP as your body floats DOWN..8 down to 7, ten times more relaxed..and SIX, ten times more relaxed..comfortably floating down, feeling good..feeling..nurtured.. feeling..comfortable .. down to FIVE, deeply relaxed ..And perhaps you'd like to know what level of trance you're at..

J: (v. quietly) U-m h-y-m-m.

C: -ok, and I'll count to three and when I say the word "State", a number will pop into mind th', you'll say that easily, and the number will be from 1 to a hundred, 50 will be in the middle, and 100 will be the deepest level of trance you can imagine, and 1 the lightest, so from 1 to a hundred after I say the word "state", 1-2-3, State!

J: (Easily-) 52.

C: Ok. And now going deeper and deeper..n'relaxing..more and more.. going down..You might see a Staircase..you (can) be on that staircase

...at some..place...Down to..to FOUR..each countdown ten times more relaxed..you get down to 0, you can be in touch with the Inner..And that staircase can be a circular staircase..go round and round..your arm'll be getting heavier..going down deeper and deeper as the arm goes down..THREE..TWO..we'll get down to 0 will be the Center of the circular staircase talking to the Inner..2..1..ten times more relaxed ..the arm's- arm moving down to zero.. getting very.. very relaxed.. we'll talk to the Inner..down, arm getting heavier..

(moving microphone out of the way) ..

.. ZERO. ..

I'D LIKE TO TALK WITH THE INNER..L'ME KNO' WHEN THE INNER ..IS
THERE.. TALK WITH THE INNER... *HELLO..*

(a Sound) **Mmm.**   *6 seconds*

..AND, DO YOU HAVE A NAME?

Jonathan - .   *(Gives full name matter-of-factly*
                                         ...Quietly, Strongly)

OK..ARE YOU THE INNER?

Um hymm.   *(Strongly and sweetly)*

OK..WHAT DO YOU THINK ABOUT UM..JONATHAN' STUTTERING?

**That..um..when he stutters, he speaks as if from under
a lot of pressure. And that he..um..doesn't want
to rush, a lot of things.**

HE'S TRYING TO KIND OF SLOW THEM DOWN INSTEAD OF RUSHING-

um hym   -WITH ALL THAT PRESSURE.

DOES HE CHECK WITH YOU, VERY OFTEN?

N-o-o.

.OK..DOES HE KNOW ABOUT YOU?

I think so.

.OK.. BUT DO YOU -KIND OF- WATCH OVER HIM?

Yes.

OK..AND HOW..HOW LONG HAVE YOU BEEN HERE?

A long-.. for years. [48]

.OK..AND HOW OLD ARE YOU? ..DO YOU HAVE AN AGE?

Umm..   (*younger tone of voice:*)

About eleven years old.

.O.K.. DO YOU TAKE CARE OF THE-

..WHAT DO YOU TAKE CARE OF?

All the..inner..thoughts.

.'K.. SO JON IS-IS -WHEN HE'S PUT UNDER PRESSURE- IS WHEN
HE STUTTERS AND..HE SLOWS IT DOWN..SLOWS DOWN
SOME OF THE PRESSURE.

Yea-.

DO YOU HAVE ANY OTHER IDEAS FOR HIM?..
BECAUSE SOMETIMES HE'S UNCOMFORTABLE..WITH THAT
STUTTERING.. SOMETIMES HE DOESN'T LIKE IT.

I think he should..make..um..should be..should..take
it e-a-s-y.

And when he..thinks he's gonna start stut-
..whe-when he starts the stuttering, he sh-, h-he
should top-stop and r-e-s-t for like fifteen,
twenty seconds.

---

[48] *since 4 year old? could be "four" or "for."*   2-1991

SO KIND OF JUST S-L-O-W DOWN, TAKE IT EASY..OK.
  WE WERE GOING TO DO SOMETHING WITH HIM TODAY ABOUT..
  KEEPING IN TUNE WITH THE BEAT..KEEPING IN TUNE WITH
  THE RYTHYM.. WOULD THAT BE OK?

Y-e-a-h.

.OK..IS THERE ANY-ANYTHING YOU WANTA-, WANTTA TELL HIM,
  RIGHT NOW?

N-o-o.

.OK..WOULD-JU- WOULD IT BE OK IF HE HAS QUESTIONS FOR
  YOU, TO ASK YOU?

Y-e-a-h.

SO THAT WOULD BE OK.
  HOW COULD HE GET IN TOUCH WITH YOU?

U-m-m..

8 seconds

umm..

5 seconds

**He should call out to me ..um ah quietly..
on the inside.**

.OK.. AND YOU'LL BE THERE. /?

Yeah.

AND YOU CAN GIVE HIM SOME IDEAS, OR SOME ANSWERS?

Yes.

OK. UMM..
  SO HE WOULD QUIETLY CALL OUT TO YOU ON THE INSIDE,
    AND YOU'LL BE THERE.

y-e-t.   *Very quietly*

ARE YOU AWARE OF HIM HAVING CERTAIN QUESTIONS THAT NEED
ANSWERING, OR-..?

yeaah..

.. -OR ANY PARTICULAR PROBLEMS- ?

nnnn.

.OK. -BUT YOU'LL BE THERE FOR HIM.

yeas.

OK. ..AND-AND YOUR NAME..AGAIN?

Jonathan - .

OK. .SO YOU HAVE THE SAME NAME. ..AND-AND HIS NAME?

Nhm, Jonathan - .

OK...AND YOU'RE ON THE INSIDE, AND YOU'LL BE THERE
FOR HIM.

CAN WE TALK AGAIN?

Yeas.

OK..WELL THANK YOU.

Nn hymm.

C: Ok now just drifting..drifting..floating..feeling very
comfortable and very relaxed..feeling in tune..breathing in
relaxation..going deeper and deeper..be anywhere you-you
wish..maybe on the staircase.. you may not be..wherever you
wish..and if it's ok, STATE..number from 1 to 100 comes to mind,
State. .[no clear response] ..'k..now just relaxing..just drifting ...soon
you'll be hearing the sound of a metronome..certain beat..and as
you're continuing to float, keep in mind that the major problem in
stuttering or stammering may be..a tendency to rush into speech..
[49]

---

[49] As just described by Jon's Inner .. the issue of rushing .. we utilized hypnotic
protocol per Dr. Herbert Spiegel, along with this Inner core work.

..or trying to slow down pressures..However you will find out that you'll be able to..relax whenever you wish..and just slow down consciously. Anytime you wish, you can count down, from 8 to any particular number on down..and each time you count down, you'll get ten times more relaxed when you wish. You can do that with numbers, inside. [An allusion to Inner's statement, "**- On the inside**"]

J: (almost imperceptibly-) **uh huh**.

C: *You don't have to do it with your speech. You'll be able to have your speech continue on .. rhythmically .. feeling very good and flowing out, with whatever you wish to say, while keeping in whatever you, don't wish to say.*

.. And soon we'll be hearing, the metronome sound..And so we're talking about the idea of following the beat.. the beat, always the beat. The important beat is the INNER beat.. your own beat.. following it.. flowing with it.. flowing around it.. slowing up.. speeding up, whatever you wish.. but always a-in mind, your own inner beat.

NOW I'D LIKE TO BE IN TOUCH- I'D LIKE TO TALK WITH THE INNER.. ONCE MORE.. TALK WITH THE INNER?.. IF I COULD. ..AND JUST CHECK IF THAT IS OK.. TO FOLLOW THAT INNER BEAT..BEAT.. ALWAYS THE BEAT..

(~)

AND IS THAT SOMETHING THAT YOU CAN HELP PROVIDE JON WITH?

CAN YOU HELP PROVIDE THAT OUTER JON.. WITH THE-THE INNER BEAT?

(~)

Ok...you can think about that.. Just be there now floating.. Coming up that staircase feeling together..knowing that you can always rely on that inner beat.

Coming up to that circular staircase..coming up..0 to 1..with ten times more energy..ok..Jon..comin up, to 2 ..ok..

AND I'D LIKE AGAIN TALK TO THAT INNER - CAN I TALK WITH THE INNER?

(very quietly:) **Hym hymm.**

WOULD THAT BE OK TO FOLLOW- FOR JON TO FOLLOW THE INNER BEAT?

(quietly) **Hym hymm.**

OK..IS THAT SOMETHING YOU'D- YOU COULD HELP PROVIDE HIM WITH?

Yeas.

OK ..WOULD THAT BE OK WITH HIM TOO?

I don't know. *(Possibly coming up on his own)* [50]

C: Ok, coming up, 2, 3, coming up the staircase, 4..5, feeling very good, and refreshed, 6, 7, 8..eyes opening, making a fist.. (Looking at the clock..) what time do you have?

J: 5:26

C: Ok. So how are you feeling?

J: Better!

C: ok

J: I felt-I felt myself starting to fall a-sleep.

C: Yeah, getting in to it..deeply..aah -so do you remember- what we talked about?

J: Umm, trying to figure out what makes me stutter..

C: ok, remember the idea on that?

J: That I'm being- th-that I don't want-a hurry up with all that stuff?

---

[50] *After all, I had just asked about what was okay with outer Jon.*   *4-22-1991*

C: Well, that was put- it was put a little bit different.. that you- that you're being pressured, and then uh yeah, that you don't want to hurry up, you slow it down?- /*J: yeah.*/ -What do you think?

J: Mm I think that's a good explanation.

C: 'k. Have you thought of that one before?

J: Nnn-, n-not really.

C: Aah. ..I think that-that's a good explanation. Nn I-I was talking with- with the Inner about, maybe there's other ways. If you want to slow somethin' down, you can slow it down, and not have to stutter. What do you think?

J: Nnn, that's a- that's also a good explana- that's also a good idea.

C: Were you aware of that Inner part of you- /*J: n-o.*/ -before? Am is that something that you, didn't have any idea about?

J: no.

C: How do you feel about it?

J: I feel good that- I- have the- have the Inner..feeling, to me.

C: You can always- always rely on it. It's always there.

J: yeah.

{*We spoke about possibly getting a metronome.*}

C: It's kinda neat. You can kind of adjust it how you want to. But it's just a stand-in. The main beat is your own Inner..inner beat. So how- any questions on how you- /*J: no..*/ Umm..so having that Inner is somethin' you weren't aware of..

J: yeah.

C: Well...any uh any thoughts on it?

J: not really.

C: Ok. ..Do you know how to get in touch- in touch with yourself or with that inner part, whenever you wish?

J: To- to call out in-in-in-in-inside sort of quietly.

C: Yeah...yeah! ..Ok, well we- ahm I'm glad I ran into you in the el- /J: yeah./ -evator out there; we had a chance to do this- this (idea). We almost missed each other.

J: yeah.

C: (chuckle) Ss- so..anything- any questions you have of me?

J: Nn-not- not really.

C: Ok, well you can let me know how, y'kno how this- how this is going- /J: ok./ -umm, and then, when shall we meet, next (week)?

J: Is Wednesday still open?

~

During closing, I wanted to carefully check out Jon's reactions thus far. I contained my positive feelings about today's session, and to monitor his reactions during the week, asked Jonathan to call me if he felt the need. We set a time. Jon left on his own, to travel home. Soon his mother and sister arrived, a few minutes too late to pick him up.

Afterwards.

Jonathan was positive & matter-of-fact about his newfound awareness of the Inner. As he came out of hypnosis he said,

"I feel good that- I- have the-have the inner feeling, to me."

I didn't want to press him about what had just occurred yet wanted to monitor any outcome with great care.

Unfortunately for my planning, Jon skipped a session or two because, as he told his mother, he just didn't need to come in. When he returned two weeks later, he was glowing!

When Jon came in, June 2, he was talking more fluently; he had done *well* with his presentation, and was happy to report he had looked at his cards only once the whole time, and he felt very good when he was done!

He said, *"This whole thing we worked on had worked."*

He felt he had no real issues right now, that school was out today, and he was looking forward to some fun next week bicycling.

Previously Jon would offer only the one-word responses, *"yeah," "no," or "I have ,, no idea."* I would have to ask more questions geared to get back even small replies. This time, as he reported no issues nor changes, he was considerably more active in communicating.

We spoke of family issues, and that he is "not getting in any trouble with mother or father. Instead," he clarified, "at times they are getting in trouble with me," for example forgetting to tell him about an appointment.

As we set up another appointment he said, "After next week my schedule is free ~ and anytime after would be fine."

We set up a time; I handed him a pen and he wrote down the time, which he said he would put on his door to make sure he remembers it. As we were concluding, he spoke for fifteen minutes about various *"interesting things."*

One of those things was a bus accident he was in on the way to the office today. He casually described what happened; he thought it was interesting, kind of funny. The bus hit the cab and knocked it sideways halfway down the street, and the cab driver and bus driver were screaming and yelling at each other. Jon thought it was pretty comical.

Jonathan asked, had I heard the news about a sniper at Belmont and Sheridan today, our neighborhood? It turned out to be a pellet/beebee gun but a sniper nevertheless. I asked how he felt about it, and Jon replied, "Well I don't want to be hit by any snipers, that's for sure."

Jon added, *"What is this world coming to?"*

He then went on a monologue, discussing the situation of a young woman in a suburb, who had killed in a rampage, a close young friend of someone he knew. A monument was put up in the park and when it was time for the memorial service, there was a bomb threat!

Again he asked, *"What is this world coming to?"* He asked this with seriousness, due concern and whimsical grace.

I responded, "These people are out on a limb--not in touch with themselves, as compared to staying under the tree and closer to the roots."

He replied, *" Definitely! "*

Jonathan's Second Inner Core contact

June 21, 1989

As per Jon's request we repeated the Inner core process for another prime concern of his--this time, *catching a baseball!*

First the Inner announced,

I am here.

~

It gave an analysis of Jon's hurry-up problem with catching the baseball and how to effectively slow this one down too.

In the next weeks Jonathan didn't mention baseball.

He came back and reported he was now able to keep up with his Father in another sport, golf.

He gleefully added with a casual demeanor,

"And I even got a hole-in-one!"

~

Over the next Year.

Jonathan's overall achievement battery score increased by a whopping *20* percentile points. [51]

---

[51] In tests, year one: Reading shot up by 41 *(15th to 56th)* percentile, Vocabulary by 24 (*62nd* to *86th*) percentile.

<u>*Over the next Two Years*</u>.

Coping with vastly differing opinions about his schooling, Jon selected high school, fought for it, and prevailed, to attend the school he determined as best meeting his needs.

He preferred to drop labels.

Effective learning ability for Jon is an acceptable, and more accurate, descriptor now.

<u>*Postscript*</u>.

Jonathan, the youngest person thus far to develop a connection with his Inner core, utilizes this inner resource judiciously to this very day.

And he awaits others to find out about it too~so they will know what for so many years he has known.

Lost

He gets confused.

<6>

Saga

On Patience

May 23rd, 1989

fighting that ... the constant feeling

of rushing, impatience ... causes rejection

Name	Age	Occupation	Inner contact	Prior therapy
Saga	34	Clerk	5-23-89	5.5 months
			1-09, 1-26-90	

*S*aga was was out of control. His life was rough
& his predictable life span short.

Of a smaller physical stature he allowed, sought or found himself in hazardous situations with various multiple partners frequently unknown to him.

In therapy for five-and-a-half months, he had progressed in certain ways but given the intractability, severity and chronicity of the self-destructive behaviors, S's prognosis was "guarded" meaning unfortunately, very poor.

With such dynamics too frequently, not much changes.

There were no other viable options! Contact with the Inner Core might offer him a way to connect to a better or to even a basic awareness.

An Inner voice explained the sexual obsession (and unknown to this writer, surfaced a healthy *shame* [52]).

This voice pinpointed ingrained patterns and reasons. While I was not entirely sure what I was speaking with during hypnosis, the ideas were clear and the outcome better than predicted.

Saga desperately required awareness.

Could hypnotherapy assist him in some way?

Following is his initial contact with the inner core.

---

[52] *This was inaudible. I could not hear the word, "ashamed" until tape was played multiple times, transcribing 16 years later.*   *4-03-2005*

May 23, 1989

S=Saga   T=Therapist

T: ..usually start like this..

S: ..eye roll, right?

T: yeah but .. before we go into the hypnosis what are the kinds of things that <u>you</u> want <u>me</u> to check out with the core, or ask about? what are the kinds of things that you'd be interested in *knowing* about?

S: About myself?

T: yeah

S: *(said very softly and quietly:)*

   .. like my actions and habits, and things like that?

T: any of that, any of the above, *(quietly)* and more ..

S: yeah..one thing that *(small titter)* sticks out in my mind   to be truthful is , ummm ... ummm there is still a little of that desire in me to ah. ..

I love JT okay? but then when I miss him, and the loneliness and I feel like when he's not there..then I'm attracted to somebody else...and I don't *want* to be. I want to be able to *wait.*

T: yeah .. it's about what to do about.. well more than what to do ..

S: w-well I've been saying "I need more activities to do .. when he's not there" and he knows that he says, "Well I can't be there all the time .. so you got to, y'know to take care of business while I'm not here."

T: So you want to know something about how to relate to others.. attraction and sexuality issues, that you've been dealing with a long time ago, some time ago, a lot..

S: ummm, well I know I've been doing that a long time, over years and it's hard to break that habit. I know that he's in my life and I love him very much. but I could leave here right now and looking at.. God!

T: And what do you want to know about that?

S: I want to.. not look at 'em sex.sually .to not look at them sexually but just appreciate them .. in the way that they look and they are, I guess, just a masculine figure..

T: Can you just *appreciate* them sexually? or not..

S: ..by looking at them?

T: yeah .. well maybe that's an issue, 'is that okay? is that not okay? or..'

S: .... I'm not sure because I'm starting to, starting to *(titter)* look at them .. Before, if they were close enough to me I might start flirting or something like that .. Now I'm not someone .. I'm afraid to do that. Because_desire to do it. I guess I am appreciating them because I can't get that close.

T: yeah.. so.. you want to know about the de<u>s</u>ire to do something about it. Not just.. You partly want to know about what's involved in the attraction or the appreciation. But also your concern is the desire_and doing something about it.

S: right.

T: Is that generally it? Because I want to get this as close as I can to .. to what you .. you want me to check out.

S: Okay, , Umm .. umm .. yeah .... hopefully ..

T: sounds like there's more..

S: Okay, yeah *(laugh)* .. there is.

Okay there's this guy I know, he works at the office. We always talk and we go home on the bus together and everything..

So this weekend JT wasn't there... so I met him .. outside, and I invited him up and we..we fondled a little bit,—*(said quietly)* we had sex .. so normally I would feel real bad .. but I don't because it was mutual. And it was ..safe.. but I wondered, why did I do it?

What made me... go that far .. when I knew that maybe TJ would be there tonight? So that's the whole story.

T: yeah .. so this was recent .. yesterday or?

S: Sunday..

T: Sunday?

S: Yeah *(relieved to admit,)* Sunday.

T: after drinking?.. did drinking play a part of it?

S: Yeah drinking was involved .. just two.

T: ..think that had something to do with it? ..even though it was just two..

S: It increased the depression..even though my buddy had just left .. my aunt was home all day.. So it should have been a full day. I should have been satisfied. Omm.. I wasn't satisfied sexually.. maybe that urge..wasn't satisfied..

T: was JT pulling back?..you say you had the whole day..

S: he was pulling back ..

T: because I was .. could have this been a way of working something out..umm..in life (actions) rather than going back and working it out with JT, and the relationship.. well, I don't know these are *questions* ..

S: Yeah

T: well, you know, you say you didn't feel bad, there are some *questions* you have about it, like why?, but the plus was that it was mutual and it was safe .. safe sex.

S: It was something that, if I didn't know JT, I would want to get together with the person. That's why I say, mutual.

T: yeah it would have been a more personal ..

S: right. Rather than getting *real* bombed out and having *anybody* ..

T: So this was more .. /*S:* I wasn't../ *T:* ..*human.*

S: I wasn't really drunk.. I was aware .. very much aware. So maybe I'm taking some heart, huh? on myself. .. maybe? .. I thought about that.

T: it..depends..well those are questions to ask .. the Inner..

S: yeah/ *T:* ahh.. /but then on the other hand, I say_I did stop - I stopped in the middle - instead of y'know, keep going through the whole weekend..

T: *(misunderstood some details..)*

S: right .. yeah .. well..

T: Well, let's .. _ get to the Inner. See what ..

S: well ..

T: I think you'll get somme.. more clear answers than I can give you. _

..my point of view, it sounds like..it's certainly much better than what you've experienced before. In terms of drinking .. a lot of drinking involved .. and maybe not drinking involved, and then sex indiscriminately .. then feeling miserable about it. /*S:* right..yeah../ ..and at great risk to you physiologically /*S:* um hymm/ as well as .. hurtful to you /*S:* um hymm/ .. psychologically.

S: Yeah, that's exactly true.

T: So this is sure a *different* place than that. So the question is, where are you in your relationship to JT? where do you want to *be*? And do you want to be monogamous?

96

or or do you want to be ahh .. ahh.. a little more.. little more open relationship? Then it..it really depends on...

S: I want a monogamous relationship. um umm ..

T: ..and what messages you're getting from him.. well shall we do the..

S: we better get to this before you run out of time ..

T: okay, yeah.   *(Quite true.)*

{Getting set, setting up the footstool}

T: and "1".. are you comfortable? both arms balanced out on pıllows?..okay..both arms resting comfortably, and getting yourself set, very comfortable..and "1" looking up, towards your eyebrows and towards the top of your head .. and "2" ... okay.. and "3," *breathe..relax and your body floats down .. while your arm floats up. More relaxed ---*

Eight .. down to the seven, 10 times more relaxed , 6 .. you'll be going down a circular staircase .. it may be blue.. it may be any..various colors...when you get down to the bottom of the center of the circular staircase you'll be in touch with the Inner.

Going down to "6" and "5", 10 times more relaxed, when you get down to zero. You'll be in touch with the Inner at the center of the circular stairway. . that we'll be in touch with the inner .. "6" to "5" .. "4" deeply relaxing .. and nurturance and care of the body .. and breathing it in .. and breathing it through out the being. And I'd like to know what level of trance from 1 to a 100 - 50 the average.. and "State"?!

S: *(very very quietly)* Ummm .. umm .. .. "36"

.. okay.. now just allowing yourself to float ..

Easier and easier .. focus on the sound of my voice .. any thoughts, any extraneous thoughts float off .. float off to the side.

You can let yourself float .. and at the same time find it easier and easier to focus on the sound of this voice .. on the meaning of the words..of the thoughts.

Going deeper, and deeper, dripping off.. drifting off ..from "4" down to "3" .. deeper .. and deeper. Any other sounds just fade away...float away. Any extra thoughts, or other thoughts..letting them fade away..float away.

Find a comfortable place .. meanwhile going down that circular staircase .. circular staircase. "4" to "3" .. relaxing.. "3" to "2" .. any tension disappears and floats away .. "2" to "1"..Going deep. Sleeping. Relaxing ..

"1" .. and "0!"

I'D LIKE TO TALK WITH THE INNER.

LET ME KNOW WHEN THE INNER IS THERE ..

AND HELLO ...

| 7 seconds

bhy me   *Indistinguishable..extremely quiet*

HAVE YOU BEEN..LISTENING TO WHAT...THE OUTER , WHAT S. HAS

    BEEN SAYING..PREVIOUSLY..ABOUT HIS CONCERNS?

yes   *Said with great comfort,*
                              Melodious.

   ...K'

WOULD IT..BE OKAY FOR US TO TALK ABOUT THOSE?

Yes.

FIRST, WHAT IS YOUR NAME?

S..   *possibly young?*

AND.. AHH, HOW OLD ARE YOU?

thirty-five

98

K', AND.. WHERE ARE YOU?

I'm in Dr. Brickman's office, in a therapy session. [53]

AND AM I IN TOUCH WITH THE INNER?

yes

O.K. AND HOW LONG HAVE YOU BEEN WITH.. WITH S.?

Om .. 35 years.

NOW HE HAS SOME..SOME CONCERNS.. ABOUT SOME ACTIONS AND HABITS ..AND WHAT TO DO ABOUT THEM.. PARTICULARLY ABOUT ATTRACTION..AAHM TO VARIOUS PEOPLE. SOME THOUGHTS ON THAT?

emm He does.. em.. He gets confused. He doesn't understand why. mm, why his mind goes to those mm.. thoughts. mm.. at random.. mm. at any time .. mm

..SO HE GETS CONFUSED ABOUT THAT

.. em hm..

WELL, WHY .. WHY? - OH..YES?

mm.. Times when he shouldn't think about that .. mm when he's concentrating on something else and the other thought slips away. mm omm

(very faint)

Then the attraction towards a male body mm, even a face umm mm mm.

It's the control of the.. thoughts.

HE WONDERS WHY HE HAS THOSE ATTRACTIONS .. IMPINGING ON HIM..IMPOSING ON HIM.

right, imposing ..

A MALE BODY, OR A MALE FACE..

mm .. It's the control of the..thoughts.

---

[53] *I questioned how deep he was in hypnosis; and was this the inner core? (He persisted with using 'Dr.' years before the degree).*   2-3-2005

HE WONDERS WHY HE HAS THOSE ATTRACTIONS .. KIND OF,
IMPINGING ON HIM.

   ...

He feels that something else is more important, that
should have all his attention..

(*Repeating*)

He feels that something else is more important, that
should have all his attention..

SO WHY DOES IT IMPOSE, OR DOES IT IMPOSE?

 It imposes, because it takes him away from another
  thought..

IT TAKES HIM AWAY FROM ANOTHER THOUGHT..

                              mm mm mm mm ..

 .maybe in the middle of planning something

                    .. mm mm mm ..

 Like a diversion.

SO THE THOUGHT CAN BE LIKE A DIVERSION **mm** *OF SOMETHING*
 ELSE THAT HE'S DOING. **right** *.. OR CAN IT BE A DIVERSION*
 FROM ANOTHER THOUGHT?

 Possibly.   *mm* **ahh** ..[54]   *slowly,*
                                              faintly

IS THERE A PURPOSE FOR THAT DIVERSION?

mm mm **I don't know.**

 unless it's to keep from thinking about something.

ARE YOU AWARE OF WHAT HE'S TRYING NOT TO THINK ABOUT?

        mm mm mm hym hymm ..

 yes   *mmm*

---

[54] *My own time pressure notwithstanding, I needed to s-l-o-w down more.*

IS HE AWARE OF THAT?

Not all the time.

WOULD IT BE OKAY TO TELL HIM, AS YOU'RE TALKING WITH ME, OR TO TELL ME?

I can tell him. OK
I think it's rejection! *mm and it's umm ..*

HE'S AFRAID OF .. REJECTION ..

hym .. **past rejections**
PAST REJECTIONS

and *mm.. mm..* **and impatience .. rushing.**
EMMM

Rushing. That's it. I'm fighting with the rushing .. a constant feeling of rushing.

SO YOU'RE FIGHTING, THE CONSTANT FEELING OF RUSHING.

Fighting that, the constant feeling of rushing, impatience.. that causes the rejection.. of another person, an ex-lover or a present lover.

AND THEN ANY .. ANY OLD REJECTIONS?

mm **r i g h t .. mm ..** [55]

Breathing in

WILL HE COMMUNICATE WITH YOU? RATHER THAN KIND OF ..IMMEDIATELY RUSHING OUT AND DOING SOMETHING ..

WHAT ABOUT HE COMMUNICATING WITH YOU, OR YOU COMMUNICATING WITH HIM? SO HE CAN WORK THIS OUT.. WITH YOU.. **No ..**

---

[55] *Could barely hear this. Had run out of session time...now rushing a bit myself. Would have been useful to pursue the thoughts further.*

DOESN'T HAPPEN?

No.

..WHAT HAPPENS?

He rushes out.   *'and umm*

HE DOESN'T LISTEN TO YOU.

n o

CAN YOU..BRING IT UP?

Righht, I can bring it up... but I don't let him win ..
because at that time he feels like there's ..
nothing wrong.

WELL YOU TRY TO, THE THING WHERE HE DOESN'T..WIN.
BECAUSE HE FEELS COMING OUT... FINE.. WHERE YOU FEEL IT'S..
NOT SO GOOD .. AND HE IS DOING SOMETHING WRONG, FOR HIM..

SO HOW DO YOU NOT LET HIM WIN?

By doing, taking the action.. whatever it is.   *mm*
drinking, sex .. *mm mm mm* .. anything to deviate
from being patient and waiting.. for, what he
really wants.

SO HE TAKES THE ACTION , UMM DRINKING OR SEX .. OR
ANYTHING THAT ..

It's like something has to fill in that space .. to fill in
the space. But he doesn't take time to .. sort it all
out .. think of positive things.

CAN HE ASK YOU ABOUT THIS? ABOUT THESE THINGS? CAN HE
COMMUNICATE WITH YOU..?

mm mm mm   I don't k n o w.

SO THAT'S DIFFICULT. MAYBE THAT'S ONE OF THE THINGS THAT
NEEDS TO HAPPEN..OR COULD HAPPEN, A WAY OF COMMUNICATING
BETWEEN YOU AND HIM, OR, BETWEEN HIM AND YOU. OR BOTH.

There seems to be a problem.

There's no ... " Core. " *(Smile)*

there's no solid answer that we both can be able
to agree on, and be strong with...to keep it,
There.

WELL YOU ARE THERE. HE MIGHT NOT REALIZE IT,,
BUT HERE YOU ARE. ...ARE YOU THE CORE?

Yes

I'm the core and he's.. he is another *(Small laugh)*
..an other person.

HE DOESN'T CHECK IN WITH YOU. HE'S AN OTHER PERSON.

Sometimes..

SOMETIMES HE'LL CHECK IN.. BUT HE'S ANOTHER PERSON.

..When he gets tired, or, feels sorry for himself.

WHEN HE SLOWS DOWN ENOUGH **yes** THEN HE CAN CHECK IN
WITH YOU? **mm** ..

Maybe after..the waiting period,, After the period
where he wasn't strong enough to, tell the difference
or have the patience. Or when they come as one.

UM HYMM

WOULD IT BE OKAY TO COMMUNICATE MORE WITH ME?
GET BACK IN TOUCH?

Yes

WOULD IT BE OKAY FOR YOU TO COMMUNICATE WITH HIM ..
yes ..MORE AND MORE? A LITTLE BIT HERE AND A LITTLE
BIT THERE ..MORE AND MORE

right.

..GETTING IT TOGETHER, MORE COMMUNICATING..

Right... because it's like two different people.
And umm, one's not satisfied with the other.

The one that um. has.. sexual desires, they're not
understood by the other one..

WHICH ONE IS NOT UNDERSTANDING OF WHICH ONE?

The core is not understanding why the other one does..
umm, different things.

SO THERE'S MORE TO TALK ABOUT HERE..MUCH MORE..MORE
COMMUNICATING..

FOR NOW WOULD IT BE OKAY TO .. JUST .. BE THERE .. AND DRIFT
.. AND RELAX, AND WE'LL TALK SOME MORE..

Yes

OKAY .. IN THE FUTURE?

yes

OKAY. THANK YOU.

Just drifting now .. deeply relaxing .. sleeping .. allowing
yourself to float comfortably..and finding that point anywhere
on the circular staircase ..

of "zero" up to the "1" and to"2" ..

And very comfortable .. and with your permission I'll say
"state" and what number comes to mind?

5

ok, just drifting up now.. umm umm .. finding a number on
the staircase at any particular point, what number do you find
on the staircase?

6

okay.

. .

Coming up, bringing the relaxation with you, "3" .. "4" ..
bringing the energy up "5" "6" "7" and "8" .. three getting ready,
.. your eyes closed, looking up, making a fist with the hand that is
up, two getting ready, and one, making a fist and letting the hand
drift down, and the arm .. as the eyes open.

T: Okay, now you're back to the usual State...but maybe
    somehow feeling different ..

S: yem umm

T: How are you feeling?

S: Clear .. (Laugh)! S.'s not so far over there, now.
    He's a little closer.

T: S., the core?

S: Yes, the core is not so far away from the wild one..
    Now I can think about the situation..

T: So right now you're feeling in closer proximity..
    How was it when.. the core.. when the Inner was talking?
    how was it for you?

S: It was umm   *Horn goes off in background, 7 seconds*
    It wasn't totally relaxed. ...

S: Maybe He was umm taking blame for the other ..
    a bit *(could not hear this,)* *..ashamed* ..the other's actions
were not in control as much as I feel right now.

T: He was sensing ..? or you were sensing what..
    he was feeling..?

S: I was sensing the hurt he may be putting on himself..by
    not thinking..clearly or being patient. Going too fast.

S: .. I was sensing that, the Core was sensing that

S: And yet the core felt responsible.

T: All the way you're talking..sounds like.. you are the core. .. right now.

S: well, I feel *more* like the core than I did feel before. And umm.. that's Great!!   *(a healthy laugh)*

T: well-   *S:* That's really great, Thanks.

T: well, I'm glad we had a chance to get to that today,

S: Thanks.   -That was remarkable.

T: -and you're welcome!. Thank you..for sharing that, too.

T: you have a contemplative look right now, what's that?

S: Cause I always knew .. I'm always thinking that I do have two personalities, and, they get out of control .. one gets out of control and goes crazy ..wow .. not in the sense of being a real wild person, but..forget about priorities of patience.   And all the good things. . that I *need. ...so bad*!

T: well you needed this kind of thing, and here it was. You really made contact .. with it.

~

S: [begins a new discussion, about the numbers "5" and "6" for unknown reason, and in great detail..]: [56]   *2 minutes* "... because I was already coming up ..faster.." *etc.*

S: ~ I was on my own, that's what it was ..

T: .. Confusion .. can be.. very healthy.

---

[56]   *Was this about Saga still remaining in touch with Inner core?*
(A side note: Editing in 2005, Saga is #6 ~ was going to be #5
before John G. was rightfully moved back into second.)

~

A contact with the Inner core provided information and insight, the hows and whys about confusion and random thoughts, and the rejection and impatience.

Insight included dynamics of attention distraction.

The Inner and Saga, in signature complex fashion, seemingly brought forth during awakening..an integration of both for a time.

He began moving toward balance and recovery.

~

As he became more settled with himself, Saga legally took custody of his youngest sister, to provide for her a more secure home than she had known ever before.

He stayed with this noble task for many many years.

Hidden

Buried.

<7>

Katrina

Why.

May 25th, 1989

.. find me ..

Name	Age	Occupation	Inner contact	Prior therapy
Katrina	22	Technician	5-25-89	17 months

*K*atrina was a bubbly vivacious twenty-two-year-old never at a loss for words.

During the day she was an effective nurse technician, but when not working, Katrina was gripped with anxious insecurity about mind and emotions occasionally bordering on terror.

Obsessive worrying and rumination were at least in part related to her high abilities in hypnosis. Many of her concerns were based upon having no awareness about this gift.

Traditional talk psychotherapy and hypnotherapy resulted in gradual progress, her feeling better, completing therapy and then every three months, relapsing.

Each time we would delve into Katrina's hypnosis abilities as a positive, her understanding would grow, as would her self-acceptance. Prior negatives turned positive.

Then, regression. As she put it, an *autophobia* would take over--a fear of self and what goes on inside. After seventeen months of this modis operandi, Katrina agreed to attempt something new and different--hypnotic contact with the Inner core.

~

We begin to begin the process. It takes quite some time to start the hypnosis. During preliminaries, Katrina conveys the thoughts and style of thinking which so often plague her.

In contrast to her typical flow of talking, her Core is quiet, calm, peaceful, and succinct. These differences are clear: in her verbiage, cadence, philosophy and perceptions.

The Inner will focus Katrina's multiple concerns into one basic childhood perception, her mother as being either "very strong" or "very weak."

May 25, 1989

K=Katrina   C=CB

K: a- *[breathing in]*

C: ..We'll get used to it- *[the tape recorder]*

K: ok. *[small laugh]*   *C:* -very quickly.

C: Um, so in terms of what..what you'd like me ta..to- get across- to the Inner from you- or get across to you from the Inner- do you have any..ideas on that or what your concerns are?

K: Like, w-why I fear it -y' know- why I fear somethin' like that.

C: Ok, why you fear-- ?

K: Like stupid things like that, like you know, like, like people going crazy [small laugh]- *or actually like it's, like, things that I re- like when people get para- Like ok for example* [inbreathe], *um me and my friend- my friend told me that she took a psychology course and- /C:* yeah/ *-it affected her too, it kinda scared her.* [talking more quickly] *She was reading on - it said like - and she read somethin' about a person know who was just like her* [fast:] *and she said "Oh-my-God that could be me I could turn crazy." and she said she was /C:* -hym-/ *scared for a long time but unlike me she read through the whole thing. She was very curious. I'd- stopped because it scared me so much. And then- ok, so I came over to her work, -*

C: -So she still stayed scared but she /*K:* yeah,-/continued through the whole thing.

K: -exactly and I don't think she took it as hard as me.

C: -But she did have that medical student syndrome..

K: -Right, exactly, but me I had it much worse. I actually was paranoid about it. *And the thing is that -um- she had -she was reading this magazine- she goes "Oh-my-God I gotta show you this thing about paranoia; it kinda it like freaked me out." [fast] And I'm like, "ok", in my mind I knew I shouldn't read it but I was like curious about it. So I read it /C: -y-/ and it was like this thing about these famous people that, like killed themselves because of..things -ok, because they (were depressed)-*

C: [slower] -a wonderful article to read, right?

K: Right!, so then I read about this one lady..who -like left a note and she killed herself because she was paranoid that her refrigerator was spying on her. [high, fast voice] Ok?! /C: -h-/ Now, stuff- the things like that!! like I was like "Oh-my- god-that's- "

C: -that her refrigerator was spying on her. [slower]

K: On her, yes- / *C:* yeah-

K: -so she was paranoid about that. And this other lady who was like supposedly-

C: I could see spying on the refrigerator if you're worried about food but-

K: Right- / *C:* -not the other way around.

K: -but her [laugh] refrigerator was actually spying on her ..and I was like- it was funny but it was stupid but it scared me; I was like- if you concentrate-

C: Even though it's so far out of your- /*K: out of mind, yeah-*/ -your experience, -I mean you have never had the experience of- /*K: no,*/ -refrigerators- /*K: no, no-* / -spying on you..

K: -but I [loudly] -if I like concentrated of-of- really scared of like say be like 'Well God if I really think about it-' I could actually become afraid of that too, Just like her!, because-

C: You'd have to work on that one I think..wouldn't you?-

K: -Yeah but of cou- be-cause of the fact that I could do things like that like I could- like remember my headaches? like for example? I concentrated so much on my headaches I had it every single day until I stopped thinking about my headaches; that's-   /C: -yeah./ when it went away.

C: yeah.

K: -because I have the ability to think like that, and it stays with me.

C: Well. You have the ability to do that- but you'd have to work awful hard to do that with a refrigerator./! / K: ok. /

C: You can do that with your own.. m-mind and your own headaches and..so on.-

K: right, but how about- ? ok, how about- ?

C: -but a refrigerator? have you been able to do that? -

K: -no-o but how 'bout- ? -It scared me though. It actually [slower] *for a few minutes it was like 'Stop! don't think about it' because then knowing me- I would probably think about it because, when I read that thing about th- in psychology about people hallucinating and hearing things- That-* / C: Yeah / *scared me.*

K: -and I've-I've.. in my mind I was like 'God which one would be worse?' and I thought 'hearing things would be worse' so I was s- more- so I thought about- scaring myself more with like the hallucinating thing- So then I was /C: hym../ *actually paranoid like whenever I see, like say like a dot on the wall, or something like tha.. I like have to take a double look and make sure it was- You know what I mean?-* /C: yeah./ *-I wasn't seeing things. Isn't that like so stupid? Now I'm- made myself paranoid./!*

C: Well it-it's um.. /K: [slight laugh] -it's unfortunate. It's using this high skill that you have - the hynotizability - in a negative- way..um so- yeah that's stupid I guess. [quick mutual laughing]

K: [laugh, with edge of sadness] *I know.. /!*

C: -But it's also possible to use it in a smart way. Um-

K: *But it only comes in stupid ways ha- .*

C: And that's what makes you very..ah sad.

K: Hym hem [quiet nearly tearful]

C: Ah, are you sure it only comes in stupid ways?

K: *Yeah only like when I hear about things like that or like when I told you I said I was reading about that book, and like remember I told you about that man who was afraid bec- that he would go crazy- because his Dad started seeing spiders coming out of the wall?..and that /C:* yea- / *scared me because I was like- well I was so scared about hallucinating- what if ?- you know what I mean? /C:* yeah-/ *I mean that's so /C:* -Well wh- / *stupid.!-*

C: -hat are your tears s-saying right now?, um-

K: I'm pissed. [tearful laugh]

C: So it's anger? Cause you look ve.. you look sad, and yet, it's anger. / And what are you pissed about?

K: [crying] *About that.*

C: Pissed that you're.. burdened with this skill.

K: Right. [7 sec] *Tha.. I even* [laugh] *had like a dream about it..like it was so- funny. Umm, last night I dreamt that I was coming here like you know for counseling and stuff. And um* [stuffed nose] *when I came here you had two other girls here and you're like "Well, we're going to have like three on one, and we're goin do it all together"* [cough] *and I was like "Oh ok, that's different."*

And I felt kinda weird cause we we were gonna have to talk about our own..problems in front of everybody else. So then, this one younger girl that was next to me, she's like "Oh God. I hate this-" ya know "-I have so many problems.." and this, this and that..and she's going on and on like-"Well you think that's! bad." -I go, "-At least you don't have like a phobia problem like me!"

114

-And then she's like "No. Mine are worse than yours." And then I told her about mine. And she starts laughing, she's like "Oh. my God! That is so stupid. You are so right!, yours is worse." and like she goes "At least my-my problems have to do with real life; it's not Stupid things." Ahe.. [upset laugh] I was so upset!.

C: And so she agreed [uncomfortable slight laugh] with you, and that really..upset you.

K: yeah.. And then the other lady didn't really say much and then I don't know what happened- I think I got mad, and I left- and when the other lady left, you said something like "That lady had phobias." And I was like, "Oh? Really?" [ha ha] I never got to hear her story, I just heard that other girl laughing at me every minute.

C: How'd you feel when you woke up? and talking about it now?

K: Oh, I felt like [tears] "Gad- it bothers me so much I had a dream about it!" /C: 'course in a dr- / And I knew if I told anybody else, they would be like just..laughing too.

C: Hymm. ..Well is-? The difference is that in the dream someone was laughing at you, but after you wake up you realize it's your dream. So..you create- I'm not sure that's the right word - you create the dream, y-you own the dream...to some extent. ..Um, so any ideas of what that all means?

K: That it's stupid..tha-why I do it. And it's like I even know that it's my own doing but..I'm still scared of it, like I'll say like [stuffy nose], OK I won't be paranoid about it. And then like I'll just have to take double looks on things. And that's what bothers[!] me y'know. And then I'm like "Oh my God I just had to take a double look! See, there I go again!" [laugh/cry]/C:hym./-and I feel like..it's going to stay like that forever [quietly] or something like that...That I'll just always[!] be like this.

C:[slight pause/inbreathe] So these are the things that you'd like me to check out!, with the Inner- why you fear these things-

115

K: -right. [inbreathe] *And-* / *C:* these people going cra-

K: -it always- / *C:* -zy and stu-stuff like that-

K: -seems to happen worse when um -like when I'm- like I said when I'm under stress about somthin'. It almost seems like..I'd rather concentrate on that than concentrate on my real problems, because I think that this problem is bigger than the other problems, you know what I mean? [inbreathe] *Like yesterday I was with.. Tom, and I just had another..situation go on with him, and it- that bothered me! But then I think back to this problem because this is more important than that problem, cause that's with my health, you know what I mean?* [breathe in, stuffed nose]

C: That this makes the other one pale- /*K: Yeah, right!-*/ by comparison. And it's easier- /*K: right, so-* / to deal with.

K: -yeah, so I'll concentrate on this much more, and then that's when it bothers me much more, you know what I mean?..

C: That's one of the advantages to th'..to the outer life problems- is they don't seem so big.

K: They never [!] *do when I start thinking about this- it's so funny. It's unbelievable.*

C: That's like the younger girl saying- something about the outer life problems.. versus the inner life problems...And then laughing about it - I think sh-she might have had an interesting point - until the laugh.. you know..

K: Yeah, you're right. I guess that's right!

C: -And maybe even with the laugh, [very quietly] there's some kind of..point there.. /*K:* [sniffle in]/ ..'cause, you know..

K: Really. Exactly, that's- just how I said it, that's what the girl said to me in the dream. That's because I was thinking about it earlier,Because I knew that's what I did, I kind of like..focussed so much more on my stupid things, than really-you know-..focussing on the problems.

C: [inbreathe] Well let's- /!

K: Because whenever I think about that Tom situation I get so frustrated, and it's like I can't even deal with it. It's like I don't want to think about it! Because it'll be an ongoing situation that will be either forever, ha..

C: So if you stay with him, or I mean get with him /? - are you back with him or not?-

K: [inbreathe] *No. We had a talk even and it's like- And like, y'kno' I talked with him Monday, I'm like "That's it! I don't want to even be your friend any more; I don't-* [faster] *like I don't want to talk to you for awhile. I want to see what I want because it bothers me so much when I talk to you." I get jealous; he gets jealous about what I do, and..he says he still loves me and he misses me and- but yet, "we're friends" And I told him like, what is it? what's wrong with you? he's lik' "I'm not ready to get in another relationship" he goes, "but I want you- y'know it it's nice to know you still care and 'cause I want a- I want a future probably- in the future but not now!"*

But he's just having me there- like for his convenience, for his security I think. He calls me all the time, like as though we're still going out, that's how much we call each other.

C: yeah.

K: -and he calls me -

C: So it's hard to stick with your idea of saying "I don't want to be your friend- /K: right./ -right now, or- period."/?

K: hym hymm.

C: Um, and that sounds like the outer kind of stuff, you kno' like it's hard to keep-keep centered, where you want to be with this,-

K: Right, it's- / C: -it changes the next day..

K: It does! And then, like I'm like, Ok, I'm not-

C: ..or the next minute.

117

K: - yeah exactly the more we see each other he wants to kiss me and this and that. [talking faster] *He never ask-es to see me tho; he-we always talk on the phone and I just- and I drop by his house, just to say Hi. But not to do things, but every time we see each other, it's like, something always has to happen. He has to kiss me, or whatever, or try things, and it's like "I thought we're friends," y'kno' I'm like, "that's- let's not do that anymore, we're friends."*

And we see each other, it happens again!-

C: Well there's been no-

K: -Y' know?

C: trans- not enough time of a transition if you- even if you want to be friends ..from um boyfriend-girlfriend to suddenly, "friends." There might need to be a time apart.

K: And everytime I do that tho he calls me like "OK. I won't talk to you." Th-, "give me time I wantta, I want ta think." /C: Hym./ He called me the next day at work three times. He called me at my house. He's l' "it's important, it's important - call me, call me." And, God- I went to the bars that night and stupid me called him when I came back, I'm like "what's so important?" And- you know?! [slight laugh], and then we talked again.

C: [slower] Yeah well- let's- [!] let's use the-the smartness, and the..positive..element of being as hypnotizable as you are to ah, to get to that part of yourself that really knows..what's going on. Um.. [inbreath] and also to give you that centered..feeling. Have you ever looked for that part in your self- ?

K: -what do you mean?-

C: -before? that Inner part?

K: Like that one time I said, u-u-uh like when it first happened to me when I was sixteen [first upsetting dissociative experience] *and then that it took time for me to get over it, and then I told you, remember I was like so super-strong, and stuff like that..* [in a prior session]

118

C: Oh you- you made a switch from-

K: -Yeah. / C: -very..um- / K: -from-

C: .. vulnerable to very super-strong.

K: Right. / C: um..- / K: I've never done that-

C: ..super tough! - I'm not sure that's the part that I'm talking about.

K: No because that part knew everything ( ) about me.

C: Oh-?, when you did make the switch- /K: yeah. I was- /C: -to very tough?-

K: -I was so self-confident, I mean I thought I could handle any kind of problem - and I could, too..

C: Was it- was it umm knowing everything and kind of.. shutting off your heart?

K: It was just like knowing everything but not let it get to me that much. Like you know, like say like, I remember at one time I broke up with a boyfriend, like and I cried all day, and then my aunt said something like, "Katrina, no guy's tears-" ~ "..no guys are worth your tears." And I was thinking about him like, "You're right. That's the last time I'm ever going to cry for him!" And that was the last time.

C: At what age..was that?

K: I was like..seventeen.

C: Now was that when the tough part..came out? *K: Yeah, that was when I was tough..then.*

C: So how long was that tough part..? *[covered previously]*

K: [This remained nearly two years - until a time her mother, brother and sister "went away." She was having boyfriend problems; her father began to travel too ~ leaving her all alone ..]

K: ..Then all of a sudden just one day after he left, I was crying and had a headache, and it was time to go to sleep..Then I was in bed and I was so scared; it was like "Oh my God I got a headache and it's taking me a long time to sleep. This is going to happen all over again." And because I said that, it did happen all over again.

[After the two years of a "tough" or "strong" part, Katrina experienced a reemergence of "weakness."]

K: -and ever since then I've never gotten my full self- confidence 'cause I was always scared of it.

C: Well-..scared of the tough part?

K: No, scared that I could break down so easily-

C: Oh that you could lose it-

K: -and why I did it.

C: It might be a matter of how to find it. If you do shift over into a vulnerable part, how to get back to..y'kno' the different part you want to be. ..But I always thought that tough part was a one-up kind of I-don'tgive-a-shit about anybody else.

K: Well, it wasn't actually that bad; it was just normal, better than normal though too, because whenever I got into a fight with my boyfriend, like I wouldn't think of it as so important. I wouldn't take things as so important like how I do now.

I mean- /C: hymm./ -I just let it in a normal level. /C: hymm./ Like I remember, say I'd get in a fight with him, and I'd be sleeping and he calls me "How could you sleep after we had that big fight?!! Oh my God. Aren't you worried about it?" I'm like "No! It doesn't bother me." [little laugh] You know what I mean? Just like that.

C: Well was it the centered part, or was that ah a part that closed you off from the heart?

K: That was just me, that's how I was before, nothing really bothered me.

C: 'cause that feels a little different, to me, than how I had thought of it, y'kno' */K: hymm./* -in the past, that I had thought of it more in terms of y'kno' going from a one-down position to a one-up position. *K: right../* *C:* -and breaking other guys'.. */K: yeah,/..*hearts- */K:* -no I was jus'-/ versus having your heart broken.

K: -It was just more like-I don't know- I don't know, I just..didn't really let- Like I said, then that's- my only problems were like guy problems. Like I wouldn't really care about my.. family, like if we had fights with my family or sister or school. I didn't care about anything else but just guy problems. - Like say if I broke up with a guy, that's the only time I would ever feel depressed - ever!

C: During that two years. /?

K: It was like actually..for always, ever since like I was growing up?..Y'know nothing would really bother me as much as like breaking up with a guy. That was when I when I felt the most pain. / C: Yeah, Ok./ *-You know what I mean?*

C: But what about the tough part?

K: And that tough part too, also, I went back to normal again.. I was back to normal actually. I wasn't any different than I was before.

C: Meaning- ? "Back to normal-" ?

K: Back to normal that- before I was sixteen, and that happened to me, where I broke down. I just turned back to normal actually. I was just myself. / C: Before the? /K: *yeah../* ..Oh I see..before then..

K: But I just knew I had more power then. I had- I knew I could just like shut things out...the thinking about it.

C: Yeah. ..Well could you do that before you were sixteen?

K: I didn't really think about it, like how I did then. Because I never had to go through an experience like that before- So you think about it more afterwards, that you know you can control it- by thinking about it.

K: I didn't really think about it, like how I did then. - Because I never had to go through an experience like that before- So you think about it more afterwards, that you know you can control it- by thinking about it.

C:..Yeah.-

K: [cough]

C: Well I'll be looking for the. the Inner part, y'know kind of the core, um, and whatever that is..is whatever that is. I don't know if that is the same as what you experienced um from sixteen or seventeen to eighteen, */K: hym hymm/* -or if it's something different. But it's- it's inside.- */K: hym hymm/* -That I know-

K: -yeah..-

C: -Other than that, I don't- I don't know, we'll see.. */K:* ok. [laugh] / ..what- what's there..rather than having a preconception about it. / *K: right../* But..I'll be looking for the the inner..core part.

K: -right..ok..-

C: -So, ok, so...start with the..um- */K:* [in-breath, cough] / I'll get th-

K:: *I think it has a lot to do with insecurity too.*

{while getting the footstool}

C: Well the relationship with one's..Inner, has a lot to do with security or or the lack of security.

K: -Right..-

C: -If you know where you're at, and you can relate to it, you feel very secure! If you don't, you feel very..insecure.

K: [quietly] ..*right.* [in-breath, cough]

C: [with a smile] Well a simplified version of it- */K:* [laugh]/ but- [mumbling]-I think- I think that's probably true. Um...ok...[pause]

OK, so, would it be more comfortable with the stool?
/K: um../ Is that..alright?

K: [double cough]

{setting up}

C: So you start in a..comfortable position, with your arms resting on the arm of the couch..and the..other arm..[on the pillows]..ok..and um..at one, you look up towards the top of your-your eyebrows..and then.. towards the top of your head... / *K:* [chewing sound]/ Um (awys) would- is gum um..is that comfortable? or would it be- ?

K: Is it- ? Um, it's ok, I mean- I won't chew it [laugh]..

C: [laugh] It's just a matter of what happens as you're relaxing..if you swallow it or- / *K: yeah, ok.* / C: Ah it's ok, with me, to chew gum- [mutual laughter] it's just..what happens..if you...relax. /

K: [cough]

C: So. [outside horn] Ok. -Gee I hope that..didn't ruin the gum.

K: Oh no that's ok. I wasn't worried. [mutual laughter]

C: Ok. So..we'll start..again. *One looking up towards the top of your head..*

{Going into trance: eyes up, close, arm float up, body float down [outside horn again], *breathing in relaxation and nurturance and care, any tensions float to the side, may imagine a relaxing scene - possibly an ocean scene* [a prior choice] *in part of the awareness.*}

At the same time, you'll be..travelling down a carpeted staircase. It may be a red carpet [prior color], or it may be another color. And in this case, that staircase will be a circular staircase. And when we get down to the center of the circular staircase, I will then..be talking with the Inner..

'k so be going down now from 8 down to 7 - ten times more relaxed..down the staircase from 7 down to 6 /--

{outside noises, *let them float away if you wish- easy to concentrate on sound of my voice* - checking level of trance}

5 - 4 - 3 - 2 - 1,

LET ME KNOW WHEN THE INNER IS HERE, *I'D LIKE TO TALK WITH THE INNER, AND -0- ..TALK TO THE INNER...*

HELLO.

(slight throat clearing) **ehem.**

Hi.   *(Calm and clear voice!)*

OK..DO YOU HAVE A NAME?

Katrina.

OK..AND YOU'RE THE INNER. /?

Hm-hymm.

HOW LONG HAVE YOU BEEN..AROUND?

Forever.

OK..HOW OLD ARE YOU?

Same age.

OK..Y' BEEN HERE FOREVER..OK..AND WHAT AGE?

Twenty-two.

OK..IS THE OUTER KATRINA AWARE..OF YOU?

5-6 seconds

Y-eah.

..IN SOME WAYS?

Yes.

OK..AND IN OTHER WAYS- ?

No.

124

NO?..OK..ARE YOU ALWAYS AWARE OF HER?

3 secs

..no.

OK..SO SOMETIMES, YOU'RE..WHERE YOU ARE.. AND SHE'S WHERE SHE IS..
OK.. ARE YOU AWARE OF WHAT SHE WANTS..TO KNOW, FROM YOU?

Y-eah.

OK.. AND WHAT IS THAT?

2-3 secs

Why she fears.

YEAH. (!) ..WHY DOES SHE FEAR?

11 seconds

I don't know.

'K..SHE FEARS ABOUT... PEOPLE GOING CRAZY...ABOUT HERSELF..SO YOU
DON'T KNOW WHY SHE FEARS THAT.

[a Nonverbal response]

YOU HAD SOME THOUGHT...

Her mother.

OK.. CAN YOU..SAY SOMETHING MORE ABOUT HER MOTHER?

Was so strong. A-nd she got weak.

SO HER MOTHER..WAS SO STRONG AND THEN, SHE GOT WEAK. WAS SHE..
THAT STRONG?

Yes.

OK.. DO YOU KNOW WHAT HAPPENED, WHY SHE GOT SO WEAK?

4 secs

She went through menopause.

OH..'K. ..WAS IT WEAK THAT SHE BECAME? OR SOMETHING ELSE. /?

Depressed.

*DEPRESSED! SO IT WASN'T SO MUCH A MATTER OF GOING FROM
STRONG TO.. WEAK, BUT FROM..STRONG TO DEPRESSED- ?*

(~)

5 secs

*SO THAT'S WHY KATRINA, OUTER KATRINA, FEARS..THOSE KIND
OF CHANGES ?*

I think so.

*OK..WHAT DO YOU THINK ABOUT THAT? WHAT DOES HAVE TO DO
WITH KATRINA?*

She saw her mother almost go crazy.

UMMM... SO SHE FEARS THAT.

Yes.

[inbreath] WELL DID HER MOTHER GO CRAZY?

6 secs

Hm hym-n- not completely.

*SO SHE GOT VERY DEPRESSED AND FELT KIND OF..
A L-ITTLE CRAZY BUT NOT COMPLETELY-*

Yes.

*-CRAZY. OK. SO..DO YOU FEEL BETTER..ABOUT THIS..THAN..
OUTER KATRINA?*

In what way?

*WELL, OUTER KATRINA HAS A LOT OF FEARS..AND VERY UPSET..
NOT SURE WHY OR HOW..YOU SEEM TO KNOW MORE
OF THE WHYS. I'M WONDERING HOW YOU FEEL.*

9 secs

(no response)

126

-AND IN WHAT WAY- ? UM..DO YOU FEEL..THE SAME
TYPE OF FEAR..THAT SHE DOES?

7 secs

OR DIFFERENT?

Different.

DIFFERENT?..'K. CAN YOU..T-ELL ME HOW YOU FEEL?

11-12 secs

u-hym. Can't explain it.

OK. SO IT'S DIFFERENT.. YOU CAN'T..PUT WORDS ON IT
BUT YOU CAN SENSE THE DIFFERENCE?

Right! Hym Hymm.

OK.. SO YOU SENSE THE DIFFERENCE.. WOULD THAT
BE HELPFUL TO HER..TO KNOW- ?

Hym-

-OR TO SENSE?

To sense.

TO SENSE IT. IF SHE COULD SENSE WHAT YOU'RE SENSING..

Right.

..THAT- THAT WOULD BE HELPFUL TO HER. /?

Hym hymm.

- EVEN IF SHE COULDN'T PUT- NEITHER OF YOU COULD-
OR DON'T PUT THE WORDS ON IT-

R-i-g-h-t.

-THE-THE SENSE IS THERE.   2 secs   ..AND IT-IT'S-IT S-
IT FEELS BETTER.. SOMEHOW..DIFFERENT.

(~)   *3-4 secs*

127

UMM..IT'S- IS IT SLOWER OR FASTER?

Slower.

OK..IS IT MORE...AHM, SOLID.. OR LESS SOLID?

[v. quietly]   **Solid.**

YOU SAY IT IS SOLID? OK.. UM, CAN SHE TURN TO YOU, AND ASK YOU ABOUT THIS, AND GET THIS FROM YOU?

Hym hymm.

OK, H- DOES SHE DO THAT MUCH?

Hym hymm.

HOW DOES SHE DO IT?

3-4 secs

She ..kind of talks ..to herself in her mind.

ok..

And she still doesn't get satisfied.

DOES SHE REACH YOU?

5 secs

~ Not really.

SO SHE KIND OF TALKS TO HERSELF IN HER MIND BUT DOESN'T QUITE GET THROUGH TO YOU.

Right.

WOULD SHE FEEL MORE SATISFIED IF SHE COULD GET THROUGH TO YOU?

Yes.

OK. HOW CAN SHE GET THROUGH TO YOU BETTER?

6-7 secs

Don't know.

OK. SO NOT SURE OF THE ANSWER TO THAT..BUT IF SHE COULD GET THROUGH TO YOU MORE,...SHE'D FEEL BETTER. /?

128

Yes.

OK. ..NOW..WHAT ABOUT YOU GETTING THROUGH TO HER?

2 secs   ..HOW WOULD THAT BE?

7 secs

how

WOULD IT BE OK FOR YOU TO REACH HER?

Yes

OK..AND..HOW WOULD YOU DO THAT? HOW DO YOU DO THAT?

13 secs   (siren noise)

I don't know

BUT YOU CAN DO THAT?

I'd- I don't know.

OH YOU DON'T KNOW, OK.. [in-breath] SO THE QUESTION IS..IT'S NOT-
THE QUESTION IS HOW TO GET THROUGH TO EACH OTHER.. HOW SHE CAN
GET THROUGH TO YOU, AND HOW YOU CAN GET THROUGH TO HER..AND..WE
DON'T HAVE THE ANSWER TO THAT YET...CAN YOU GIVE ME SOME IDEAS OF
WHERE TO GET THE ANSWER FROM?

8 secs

IS THERE CERTAIN AGE?

10 secs

ss- Sixteen.

O-K. ..WHAT WAS IT LIKE AT SIXTEEN? -BETWEEN YOU AND HER?

6-7 secs

I liked being sixteen.   [a bright voice]

OK..SO YOU LIKED BEING SIXTEEN..UM, DID SHE LIKE IT?

Yes.

OK..WERE YOU- WHAT WAS..THE COMMUNICATION LIKE BETWEEN YOU AND HER?

fine.

-AT SIXTEEN?

(~)

FINE? - COULD SHE GET THROUGH TO YOU?

yes.

AND YOU COULD GET THROUGH TO HER?

yea-h.

O-K..AND HOW LONG DID THAT LAST?

'ntil the end of the summer.

OK END OF THE SUMMER..

Right.

..YOU WERE BEING..VERY..CLOSE..TOUCH.
    WHY DID YOU BECOME IN CLOSE TOUCH AT AH AH SIXTEEN?

Why were we?

(Different sound of voice in referring to we.)

YES.

We always haved.

YOU ALWAYS HAVE BEEN [IN TOUCH].

Right.

OK. ..AH AND HOW WERE YOU IN CLOSE TOUCH, THEN?

We're sure- I was sure.. about myself.   *(- outer Katrina?)*

OK. WHAT HAPPENED AT THE END OF THAT SUMMER?

10 secs

That's when it all happened.

OK THAT'S WHEN IT ALL HAPPENED...

130

Right.

..AND WHAT HAPPENED?

3-4 secs

That's when.. her fears started.

OK. ..SO AFTER HER FEAR STARTED ?

right.

-AND SHE LOST TOUCH-

yes.

-WITH YOU.

(~)

-OR WAS NOT AS IN C- IN CLOSE A TOUCH WITH YOU.

'n far from.

OK..SO VERY- VERY MUCH OUT OF TOUCH WITH YOU..

-yeh.

..AND, WHAT DID HER FEARS DO? DID HER FEARS CAUSE THAT?

yes.

HOW DID THEY CAUSE THAT?

5 secs

Made her lose touch.

OK..LOSE TOUCH WITH THE INNER. /?

Right.

OK. WHEN YSS- SOME KIND OF SADNESS ABOUT THAT.. OK.. AND YOU
  WERE FEELING THAT SS- YOU'RE FEELING THAT SADNESS TOO..

yes.

OK.. SO IT'S LIKE A RE-UNION TIME -DO YOU THINK?- THIS COULD
  BE A REUNION TIME?   *[talking to a younger place]*
-maybe.

'K..WHAT HAS TO HAPPEN TO HELP WITH THAT REUNION?

She has to find me again.

OK...DO YOU HAVE ANY..IDEAS FOR HER - TO FIND YOU?

5 secs

no.

..SO SHE HAS TO FIND YOU./?

[*quietly*]　**ye-s.**

IT HAS TO COME FROM HER?

[*v. quietly*]　**righ-t.**

O.K. [in-breath] ...CAN YOU FIND..HER..TOO?　..CAN SOME OF
THAT COME FROM YOU?

4 secs

[*v. quietly*] **I don't know**

OK. WELL YOU DO KNOW THAT SHE HAS TO FIND YOU.

[*louder*]　**Yes.**

UM.. THERE MAY BE TIMES WHEN..SHE'LL..LET YOU FIND, HER..
TOO. - IF IT'S OK WITH HER..WOULD YOU BE WILLING TO
DO THAT..TOO?

*[Said gently, I'm encouraging it a bit here - an exploratory
probe and suggestion, which did not receive a response.]*

4 -5 secs

(~)　　　　　　　　　*nonverbal* **noncommittal**

MAYBE..MAYBE NOT- ?

mmm.

MAYBE NOT.

Mmm.

OK. ...SO IT SOUNDS LIKE (BY THAT), WHAT YOU'RE SAYING RIGHT NOW, SHE'S GOING TO HAVE TO FIND YOU.

Yes.

OK. ..ARE YOU RIGHT THERE FOR HER..WHEN SHE WANTS TO FIND YOU?

2.5 secs

[*Quietly*]   -somewhere.

SOMEWHERE.. OK...CAN YOU TELL ME MORE WHERE YOU ARE?

7 secs

- no.

'K YOU'RE NOT SURE-

n-   -BUT YOU'RE DEFINITELY THERE.

[*inbreath*]   Yes.

OK..ARE Y- ARE YOU IN THE BODY?

yes.

A CERTAIN PLACE- ?

yes.   -IN THE BODY ?

WHERE, IN THE BODY?

[*Bit difficult to hear*]   buried deeply.

BURIED DEEPLY ..THROUGHOUT? ..OR A CERTAIN PLACE?

(~)

YOU'RE NOT SURE BUT YOU'RE THERE-

hym hymm.

-AND YOU'RE BURIED DEEPLY.

[*Very Quietly*]   yes.

OK. CAN WE TALK AGAIN..SOMETIME?

yes.

133

IS THERE ANYTHING MORE THAT YOU WANT ME TO SAY TO HER?

4 secs

[*Sweetly/ Quietly*]   **To find me.**

YOU'D LIKE HER TO FIND YOU.

yes.

OK.   *'K WELL THANK YOU.*

[*Whispered*]   - *y* -

Ok now just..comfortably floating and relaxing... breathing in nurture..comfort...feeling lik-..feeling whatever you wish..you know..the way that's best for you to feel it... comfortably floating, floating down ...breathing in relaxation and comfort..finding that circular stairw- case..going from 0 to 1 - to the 2..feeling very fine, pulling together, feeling good.. ..moving together up that circular staircase..wherever you wish ..when you get to 8 you'll feel..very relaxed and energized, bringing back some, some knowledge..ah some feelings, kind of a gift, perhaps, from yourself to yourself.. moving up the staircase 2 to 3 to 4 - 5 - 6 - 7, and 8.

{eye roll, eye opening, making and opening fist as arm [which is up] ..floats down}

K: [cough] - umm.

C: So how are you-, how are you- ?

K: How do I feel?

C: yea- / K: ok- *[cough, moving, exhale]*

K: How long *[laugh]* have we been doing this for- ? [laugh]

C: Well let's see-   / *K:*-was it short long?/ *C:*-when we started- it's two minutes to three, I think we started about- ..how long's it feel?

K: O- I don' kno' I just looked at the clock just now, it's like "wow it's three o'clock already.." *[laugh]*

C: How long do you think it- was?, or a guess.

K: hm - five minutes!/?

C: 'five minutes..'

K: Was it?

C: I think a little longer.

K: Oh *[a real laugh]*. OK *[laugh]* .

C: It means you really got into it. */K: [laugh] / C:* Because you have the different time sensation. I think it was about fifteen to twenty.

K: wow..

C: We can always y'kno' check it out sometime- */K:* yeah. / -by playing it. */K: [laugh] /* ..What do you remember?

K: [deep exhalation] I don'kno' I guess I was crying. *[laugh]*

C: Do you remember some of the ideas?

K: [inhalation]

C: You remember the crying; you remember some of the sadness.

K: [slower] ..y-e-a-h. *[clears throat; inbreathe]*

C: what else?

K: ..umm..

C: At first it sounds like- looks like, "not sure" exactly.

K: yeah I don't know- umm!, maybe. *[inbreathe]*

C: But the more you think about it, the more you might- more of it might come back..

[Was encouraging but not pressing her to remember.]

135

K: *[7 sec, laugh, sniffle]* I don't know..*[nervous laugh]..* [sniffle] ..Wait a second - wait - I can't forget. (al-)..umm! ...Oh, I have to find myself. *[laugh]*

    C: Ok.. / *K:* Oooh. *[laugh]*

    C: That was the message, **"Find me."**

K: Well how did I forget somth- *[laugh]* ? / C: well it was- / -because I knew I was doing it, umm-.

    C: well it was..a different part, easy to explain "why"...and it's how to stay in touch..y'kno', cause you always were in touch, up until sixteen..remember that?

    K: y-e-a-h.. *[inbreathe]*

    C: ..and th' s- there was some sadness there about, y'k..not being in touch..

K: I kno! *[Freer laugh]* / *C:* ..and yo'r Inner was saying "it's up to you"..to find her...

    C: So you know about that?, being out of touch.

    K: Right..I do. *[still awakening]*

    C: Well c- ..you know..I guess we got to stop but-
      /*K:* yeah, ok./

    C: -can you see any uh..benefits to your gift? from this.

K: I can, but it's just- I have to learn how to do it, you know? stop being negative and get into positive.

    C: Yeah..yeah. ..'corse you know the more gifted people I-have.. hypnosis do have trouble sometimes remembering 'cause they go deeper [not] remember exactly what was said, and yet they find a very rich place, a rich part of themselves.

K: But I guess I f- I fin- am, it gets better like when things are going *[voice wavers]* better in my life, y'know?.

    C: Yeah.

K: B' i's lik- it almost seems like *[wavering]* its like if "could I do it?" like even though things are going bad..y'know?...

C: *[inbreathe]* ..well..yeah, i-it's easier to practice..or t-.kind of.get things going right when things are going right- */K: Right../* -but once-once */K: [breath] /* it's in place, 'h then..it's in place for you even when things go badly. ..that's when you really need it even more! -well, I don't know; you need it for both- */K: [cough]* all right./ -when things are going- */K: [in sniffle]* -great, or not going so great..

K: I don't know it's weird, everytime *[sadly]* like I get depressed, that's when it c- it pops in my mind; it's so stupid. */C: By "it"- ?/* -Even like, like y' know that, that stupid fears or whatever- */C:* ye-h/ -I start thinking about that a lot more *[talking faster]* like I sa- like */C:* ye-h/ -right when I'm going to get my period..it happens. It's.. weird. *[laugh]*

C: *[inbreath]* well..do you remember what.what was said about your mother?

K: *[long inbreath]* ..Umm..uh..about my mother being depressed. -? / *C:* And when?

K: When I was in high school.

C: And it had something to do with her.periods, in a- a way. Not- */K:* yeah../ -not her periods but.uhm.uh..

K: I mean she even felt so bad she almost committed suicide about it, a- ha-ha.

C: Hymm. ..well I'm trying to remember what your Inner said, myself- if it if it was ah PMS? or ah..ah..the "end of periods"..?

K: Oh! Um-? ..it was the "end of your period." You know..
[inbreathe]

C: -and she got very depressed- */K:* Umm hymm./ -and, you said she tried-

K: -I think so! That's what I was told I guess. That's- I guess she was going through menopause..

C: Menopause, yeah- /*K:* hym hymm./ ..so I wonder if that could bring up the fear, you know whenever your period- if it has something to do with that- ?

K: I don't know, I really don't know what it is..

C: Because we've talked about periods and PMS.. /*K:* hym hymm./ -in in a physiological /*K:* right./ sense. .But is there also a psychological sense?

K: *[5 sec]* I- I don't know..it's just..all I know is just, whenever I feel..that bad, that-that that's when it starts happening 'lot more. *[in-sniffle]*

C: -Any thoughts what you'd like to do from here? before we stop, um-

K: Like what what was *[louder]* that thing that you told me- that you showed me in that one book like to write down..do you have to write it down all- like I mean every single day? Like - cog-nitive thinking?- /*C:* Oh, yeah./ -or something like that?

C: Well that's a very different approach than this; that's cognitive therapy which can certainly help!- /*K:* Oh./ -but to me..this- this is so basic- /*K:* oh./ -this is so...that's-that's dealing with some OUTER thoughts IN- /*K:* oh./ -y' know, and this is going to the Inner. /*K:* oh, ok./ -Either can can be helpful.. /*K:* hym hymm./ Um..and..you can ah- you can use, /*K:* hym hymm./ you can use some of that too.. /*K:* hym hymm./ Do you have to do it every day?

..no. /*K:* oh, ok./ I mean the more you do it, the better if it's helping..but even if you do a little bit it can help get the ball rolling.

K: oh, ok.

C: Well, when shall we meet?

K: Should we set something, or should I call you? *[a number of recent cancellations]* With my temporary work, I don't know when I have jobs and when I don't. Should I just give you a call next week, or should I -?

C: Why don't we d- let me throw something out, see we can set something up (or)-

K: Cause I hate canceling on you, y'kno', because I know how it is, because I've worked- well I do work in a dental offices, and I know how it is when [comfortable laugh] people cancel.

C: Yeah- *[grumble-grumble]*-

K: I know it's- *[laugh]*

C: But I'm I'm kind of, y' know..I don't..say the same things about you that you probably say *[mutual laughter]* about your patients..

K: -Yeah.

C: Who am I going to say it to- anyway?

K: -the people [answering service] I call up- ? They probably know me: "it's Katrina again, Cliff.. *[mutual laughter]* "

C: Well let's see- no I don't talk to them; don't worry about that- /*K:* ok./ well we can set something in two weeks and something tentative for next week...

C: Should we do that tentatively..or-

K: Yeah. Ten- *[inbreathe]* I'm..pretty [sure about next week].. I do want to come in. *{ End of tape }*

Contact with her Core provided security Katrina sought. It had been far away from her since early teenage years. Or she from it.

Far

A Big Well

<8>

Smith

May 30th, 1989

.. letting go the most ..

Name	Age	Occupation	Inner contact	Prior therapy
Smith	38	Research	5-30-89	22 months

Smith was tough, hardheaded, unemotional
and not at all drawn to hypnosis.

Smith was a politicismo par excellence. He kept to himself; and wasn't particularly interested in feelings.

Smith was an action-oriented thinker.

He is someone who probably would not be in any form of psychotherapy, except for encouragement by his colleague who had worked with and trusted me.

Smith did suffer effects of stress. Also as with many men, he had little clue about his wife. During months of therapy, he did not talk about his "inner life" nor about hers. [57]

Smith was highly standoffish about hypnosis, imagination, visualization, meditation and "any such stuff."

In these inner core attempts, Smith is the second with a high cognitive, and very low hypnotic, ability quotient; and the first with an anti-hypnosis quotient.

Yet he generously and courageously agreed--despite sincere cynicism and mostly a lack of interest--to make an attempt to reach a so-called inner core.

The prior week, Smith said he'd consider trying to come up with possible questions.

---

[57] *At night as I edit this about my security-conscious patient, suddenly a Pop !! Computer screen goes blank...all lights go out...the room goes black. As I look out on the north side of the City, all lights except hospital, fade into darkness for some hours.*   *8-17-2010*

First we discuss his questions.

Smith goes along with partial hypnotic induction, gradually, as we utilize a fractionation technique, moving into, out of, back into a focused concentration.

As we reach the Zero point, he is not sure this is the Inner core talking ~ it may be just him. Most telling, is his own description at the conclusion of the hypnosis--what it was like.

May 30, 1989

(Initially discussing political approaches...)

S: ... seminars on low intensity strategies... of course Brown is his own man, the board isn't telling him what to do but a company man's a company man. He's using them, and they're gaining power thereby ...

CB: ...Well, in terms of this, the issues about the core. You said that you've never thought of it as a separate part, before.

S: I guess I mean "separate" in the way of uh.. well separate, two, meaning disengaged you know. I think there are two aspects, yeah there is an inner and an outer aspect. But sometimes it's hard to decide, you know what's going on, to me; I can't make a distinction between the two.

CB: yeah. Well before doing this kind of work neither could I.. particularly. This..clarifies it..and uh may clarify it further, and I would guess that it will probably clarify it further. We'll see how it works for you. Because everybody has their own thing. I don't want to put something on you that's not there, I want to see how-how it is for you.

And..uh..I have seen though in all cases, that when- when it is pinpointed it clarifies what you need to do to really..have that relationship..with yourself. And uh..and what its value *is*.

143

CB: Um, any questions that you would want to ask..the core?- um or any concerns that you have or-? 'cause that's my job as facilitator..or..

S: Gee that's kind of like uh asking the *genie*, you know?.. /*C: Yeah!*/ ..what three questions? / *C: right*/ *S:* It's tough there, I don't know- / *C: ..exactly!* /

> *Horn sounds*
> *contin.....for minutes*

CB: ..difference is it's your o<u>wn</u> g<u>e</u>nie. /*S: laughing*/ ..your very own genie.

S: (hearty laughing.) -Yes but to our question!, that's rough. ..I actually thought about that before I came <u>in</u> here, but then I - /*C: oh!*/ -I couldn't think of it. I guess things are too general.

S: I'd like to ask the core, I suppose something like uh, should I really- should I really break out of uh, use this opportunity of not being employed to break out of the situation I'm in?

> ..really go crazy and make a total change in my life, you know..? I'd like to ask the core just what- what's going on?

S: I don't know how *descriptive* things get when you're doing this? You know whether it's just a "yes or no" answer you want or.. from it, or what? ..y'kno' but it's,

I'm interested in what's going on in my martial arts.. training, and just what the problem -what the main problem is with.. what's holding me back?

CB: I'll say this: in the o<u>l</u>d days -to a few months ago- *(chuckle),* everybody who did work li<u>k</u>e this only got 'yes or no' answers .. like a finger response, ideomotor questioning:

"Yes," "No" or "I don't want to answer."

CB: I've gotten responses. I mean you have to ask specifically what you want to know..and you get specific answers.. More-much more than 'yes' or a 'no'.

S: well that's, good! It's not like talking to a computer then.

CB: No not at all. That's a surprising -maybe not so surprising when you think about it. It's very y'kno'.. *(breathing in)* -well I don't want to give you any more leading suggestions.. uh just see what it's like for you...

S: yeah!

CB: ...but that's, that..that's what I've experienced so far.. that you can get.. get more answers.. Um..so,

CB: "What's-what's going on? Should I break out of the situation I'm in, go crazy, make a total change in my life?"..um..And "what's going on with the martial arts?" Any more, specific..or general?

S: ...well "what's the main thing holding me back?," yeah.

CB: ..in advancing..?

S: yeah, in advancing, and a question like, "Where do I see the best direction to go in to advance?" _ if I can think of anything where it will be a good way to advance.you know I don't know if that's the right kind of question or not.

CB: well you need a very specialized in Genie, who really knows about all the stuff.. /S: yeah../,so what about any more specifics on breaking out.. what that means.

S: well the several alternatives, one that I really try to get out of the City, pollution and everything and try another city, maybe go back to California or someplace, should I try a real career change and say the hell with everything and maybe some training..

.. or go for a new type of job change where wouldn't have to work in these--types of jobs that I've had? That's two questions that are involved with that.

C: "Career change, training, technical, move out of the technical area .."

S: move it to some type of area, I have a technical job yet, but it would be a job or I wouldn't be out like --and stuff like that..try to move to another white-collar technical, by going to school.. / *C:* okay

C: okay well maybe that, kind of enough of the beginning!

S: Yet will that- should be kind of enough!

C: Covers covers a lot, maybe there are some other areas too..um... (quietly) maybe we can see what we will cover..okay well anything else on that like..marriage, relationships..?

S: well I suppose I could ask about that too, I don't know. but you know, let's see. Let's see if this works. --while I could ask about it, I don't know.. maybe I could ask *myself* why I think my wife is an antique collector and old lamp addict, why she acts the way she does? maybe there is another analysis there in how and how the best way would be to get her out of being an addict..I mean, in terms of accumulating antiques-- not a dope fiend nor a junkie. / *C:* okay .. *(smiles)*

. . .

C: well okay. last time we did this--hypnosis--it was a while back wasn't it?

S: Well it didn't work.

CB: We did it in '87, September 2, at least that's what is indicated *(in the notes).*

S: It had something to do with my arm raising up, it didn't work.

CB: yeah, right! we had to really help it along.. *(quietly)* and yet at the same time..let's see.. you did have some of the physical responses though, in terms of lightheaded, and then..

...(*slight*) amnesia, and then the remembering about the cutoff of hypnosis with the arm..Om so you had some responses, but not the arm. You had to help it as if it were tàijíquán, back then.

C: So okay, we'll start with comfortable positioning, and one arm resting on the arm of the couch. Here's the footstool..that okay?

S: yeah that's much better I ran this morning, my legs are really killing me.

CB: so.. got my Reebok shoes in the closet over there, still using those; well moving right along here.. okay so you start with getting as comfortable as possible with one arm resting on the arm of the couch, kind of so to make it easier, that if it's going to go up that it will help it go up.

S: It's going to hit this microphone!

C: Okay is that like, that okay? / *S:* I suppose./ I'll have to figure something to do with this microphone

S: What about like this? I'll bet that works from there.

CB: Is that comfortable? / *S:* yeah. / okay maybe it will work from there.

S: Testing 1,2. Well the light's working.

CB: so taking a couple of breaths and letting them out, just kind of like getting set..getting relaxed, I'll do the same thing (chuckle).. you're smiling..

S: well it's like getting ready for a race or something

CB: yeah, while sometimes by getting ready for or race, there's a little bit of adrenaline, at the same time, you're getting kind of clear..(quietly) and all that stuff.. you're getting.. somewhere you're not sure where, some and taking a couple of breaths in, and a couple of breaths out..okay..and we get into this, *by one doing one thing, two doing two things, and three doing three things .. looking up to the top of your head, and to..*

.. I'll kind of run through at first, it is kind of a reminder) and to *taking a deep breath and holding it in at the same time, holding the eyes up and your eyelids come down, and number three, everything relaxes and floats and your arm floats up.* And I can either help it along or we can help it along. But whatever feels comfortable for you, any preference; does it matter?

S: I can do it I suppose.

CB: I know, you can.. *(laugh)* I know you can do it. okay so *one looking up towards the top of your eyebrows, and towards the top of your hand. And you can, and holding the eyes of up, and two, while holding the eyes up, closing the eyelids very slowly, and taking a deep breath and holding it, and then three, letting the breath out, and the eyes relaxing down. And as this happens, letting your arm float up, perhaps the right arm floating up as your body is floating down..*

S: *(laughing* and awake*)*

C: "*Eyes opening again.*"*(laughing together)* What happened?

S: Well I don't know, I just have to make it go up.

CB: While I'll- I'll help it too..okay so again. /*S:*(clears throat)/ Sometimes it's good to do a..fractionating technique, if it's harder to hypnotize -you come out of it, and you go back into it. as often as you, as often as you wish. okay, so,

One, looking up, two, and three, letting the body float down, keeping the eyelids closed, as the arm floats up. The arm can get very light -and we'll kind of help it go up- deeply relaxed to a comfortable place, and then becoming more and more relaxed, more and more relaxed with each breath in, breathing in nourishment ah, care, breathing it out throughout the body.

Then breathing it out, letting any tension just floating away, and I'll, you can do this any time, this relaxation on your own, any time..

..and by counting down, you can become 10 times more relaxed, which you'll, you'll be able to do right now. Going from 8 down to 7 and becoming 10 times more relaxed, being able to breathe in relaxation, and that relaxation goes throughout the body. and finding it easier and easier, not listening to, whatever you may not be interested in, and at the same time finding it easier to focus on the sound of my voice, the saying, and the meanings of the words, senses, phrases

..easier and easier to concentrate on the sound of the voice, and imagining a staircase, it may have a favorite color, a particular color of carpeting, on it, do have a particular *color* that you see?

S: *(Sounding awake,* alert*)* uh-hum, *red.*

CB: *okay..so a staircase with a red carpet. and be going down that staircase, and with each step down becoming 10 times more relaxed, going from 7 down to 6, and letting go of the outside world, and tuning into the inside at the same time, being able to follow the sound of this voice and what it is saying, my voice. so going down the staircase, floating down, moving down it, perhaps you might like to know what level of trance you are at, what level of relaxation you are in, and particularly level of trance..*

.. so when I say the word "state," I'll count to three, and say that word, and a number from one to a hundred can pop to mind, and you'll be able to say that word, I mean that number, very easily, a number from one to a hundred, 100 being the deepest level of trance, you can imagine, and one being the lightest and 50 kind of in the middle. so perhaps you'd like to know what level of trance you are at the moment, 1-2-3 'state' -- and a number pops to mind,

S: *50*

okay. okay just allowing yourself to be, wherever you happen to be, and let yourself float there,..

and you're in that staircase. and you may notice that it's becoming a circular staircase, with a banister on either side, one side, the down banister; and the other side an up banister, very solid bannisters, very comfortable looking bannisters

it's a circular staircase, you can kind of see down it, and when we get down to the bottom and the center of the circular staircase, will then be talking to the Inner.. talking to the Inner.

okay then going down the staircase 6 down to 5, 10 times more relaxed, now 5 down to 4.. much more relaxed, letting go of any tensions and letting yourself float.. just to float, going down that circular staircase, and "state!," a particular number ? pops to mind, 1,2,3, State!

S: 7-

okay, and letting yourself float, wherever you happen to float to, letting yourself float comfortably letting go of any tensions, going down that circular staircase, and when we get down to zero we'll be in touch with the inner. 4 down to 3,..like sleeping..letting go.. comfortably floating down..that red staircase. 3 down to 2.. beginning to the center of that staircase, going deeper and deeper relaxing, .. 1 ..and: Zero

I'D LIKE TO TALK WITH THE INNER.

LET ME KNOW WHEN THE INNER IS THERE.

30 seconds

I'D LIKE TO SAY 'HELLO' TO THE INNER.

(cough)   *13 seconds*

ARE YOU THERE?

well I'm here.

OKAY. AM I TALKING WITH THE INNER?

I don't know

WELL LET'S, LET'S JUST ASK SOME QUESTIONS..
     AH, WHAT'S YOUR NAME?

Smith

OKAY. AND HOW LONG HAVE YOU BEEN THERE?

here? ~ a year?
no 'here' ~ where is here?

WELL.. WHERE ARE YOU? (quietly,) THAT WOULD BE THE FIRST
                      QUESTION.

I feel like I'm at the bottom of a big well!

OKAY, AND IS THAT- IN THE BODY? DO YOU FEEL LIKE YOU'RE
     IN THE BODY?

um-hym.

AT THE BOTTOM OF A BIG WELL, OKAY,
AND HOW LONG HAVE YOU BEEN THERE?

a long time, I guess

OKAY. AND DO YOU TALK WITH THE OUTER, THE OUTER SMITH?
..VERY MUCH?

*Well the answer that comes to mind is, **no.***

DOES HE TALK WITH YOU?

.. no.

WERE YOU AWARE OF THE QUESTIONS THAT HE HAD.., FIRST OF
ALL, THAT HE HAD TODAY, BREAKING OUT OF THE SITUATION,
SHOULD HE BREAK OUT OF THE SITUATION?

what situation?

WELL HE'S TALKING..UM SHOULD HE LEAVE THE CITY FIRST OF
ALL? IN THAT HE'S UNEMPLOYED RIGHT NOW, AND WOULD THIS
BE A GOOD TIME TO LEAVE THE CITY FOR A CAREER CHANGE?

THE WAY HE PUT IT AT FIRST WAS, "IS THIS A GOOD TIME TO GO
CRAZY AND MAKE A REAL CHANGE IN MY LIFE?"

WHAT YOU THINK ABOUT THAT?

good question.

SO IT'S A GOOD QUESTION. OKAY.

somehow I don't feel like I have the ability to answer.
I don't have enough information.

OKAY. SO THERE'S MORE INFORMATION?
THAT MIGHT BE NECESSARY.

right.

WHAT MORE INFORMATION IS NECESSARY?

well I- What the possibilities are.

OKAY.

where a person- where I'd like to go with the life,
where, where ' should be headed?

SO WHERE THE LIFE SHOULD BE HEADED..WOULD BE HELPFUL..
TO KNOW.

DO HAVE ANY THOUGHTS ON- ON WHERE THE LIFE SHOULD
BE HEADED?

my thought is to just go, just go with the .. path
that would give the best .. peace of mind.

OKAY. SO PEACE OF MIND..WOULD BE..VERY IMPORTANT.

yeah the other stuff isn't very important, really.
money, things like that.

SO WHERE THE LIFE WOULD BE HEADED, IN TERMS OF PEACE
OF MIND.. ..IS VERY IMPORTANT.
WHAT WOULD THAT INVOLVE?

I think it involves..somehow dealing with this
emotional turmoil.

'K. WHAT IS GOING ON WITH THAT EMOTIONAL TURMOIL?
-- IS THAT THE OUTER'S EMOTIONAL TURMOIL?,
DO YOU FEEL THE EMOTIONAL TURMOIL?

well I feel it now

OK. WHAT'S IT CONSIST OF, AND HOW IS IT, EMOTIONAL TURMOIL?

looks like a mass of ('dim), confusion to me.

IS THERE AN IMAGE TO IT?

it's like shifting clouds of just.. grief and.. tension
and .. gray areas of uncertainty.

IS THERE AN ANSWER FOR THAT. WHAT DOES IT INVOLVE IN TERMS
OF DISSOLVING THIS EMOTIONAL TURMOIL AND THESE CLOUDS?

I think an answer is involved, that is finding
something ('dim) to focus on like a ('dim)...

like a task or a job or something to resolve
some of the conflicts in society. helping people

SO LIKE A TASK OR A JOB COMES TO MIND LIKE HELPING PEOPLE OR
HELP THEM RESOLVE SOME CONFLICTS, SOCIAL CONFLICTS

I just really think there's this really huge burden
compre- comprehending what's going on, and
not being able to undo anything about it.

153

..and..the..working on things like that
just..are really like another form of
just dope or something.

SO THE BURDEN OF KNOWING WHAT'S GOING ON, SEEING WHAT'S OUT THERE, AND BEING STUCK- FEELING STUCK ABOUT DOING SOMETHING ABOUT IT, TRYING TO DO SOME THINGS IN CERTAIN WAYS, AND BEING ADDICTED TO..CERTAIN WAYS OF DOING THINGS.

IS THAT WHAT YOU'RE SAYING?

I feel it is not enough to just, exist.

I think it's important...to ah actively
come to grips with, physical things
which are manifestations of what's
bothering him.

And um.. you can't just be an ordinary citizen ~

..HAVE TO DO SOMETHING.. "ORDINARY" MEANS ..
NOT DOING SOMETHING?

nebish.. being a nebish.

YEAH, VERSUS HAVING, HAVING IMPACT, GETTING SOMETHING
ACCOMPLISHED.

CAN THE OUTER, SMITH STAY IN TOUCH WITH YOU
ABOUT THIS? DEAL WITH YOU ABOUT THIS?

BEFORE, THERE WAS REALLY, NOT MUCH COMMUNICATION..
GOING ON. CAN HE ASK YOU, CERTAIN QUESTIONS
WHENEVER HE WANTS TO KNOW?

I suppose so. I just don't know h o w.

HE CAN ASK YOU, BUT YOU DON'T KNOW HOW- HOW
HE'LL GET TO YOU..

right now it just seems like there's just me

154

JUST YOU AND YOU'RE STILL AT THE BOTTOM OF THE WELL?

yeah

WELL LET'S SEE WHERE WE GO WITH, ABOUT THAT.

ANOTHER QUESTION WAS, WHERE SHOULD HE GO, REGARDING MARTIAL ARTS? "WHAT IS MAINLY HOLDING ME BACK," WAS THE QUESTION, "AND ADVANCING IN IT?" -- DO YOU HAVE SOME THOUGHTS ON THAT?

WHAT IS HOLDING YOU BACK- WHAT IS HOLDING HIM BACK?

I think there's a feeling that there's no real way to overcome obstacles. that _ work ed to get to a goal.

NO WAY TO GET WHERE HE WANTS TO GO..

WELL WHAT ARE THE- WHAT ARE THE OBSTACLES?

well age is one, physical infirmities, another. ah, problems with training, lack of money.

WHAT ARE THE MENTAL OBSTACLES?

mental obstacles, not wanting to push past a certain point, holding back.

WHAT POINT IS THAT?   (a slight press)

I'd say it's the point beyond which it's a hobby, going past where it would be a hobby.

WELL THAT- THAT WAS SMITH'S NEXT QUESTION IS, "WHAT'S THE BEST DIRECTION TO GO?..WITH THAT, WITH MARTIAL ARTS."

the best direction is whatever one would lead to letting go the most.

155

AND LETTING GO OF WHAT?

notions about what's possible and what isn't.

*OKAY. ONE OTHER AREA THAT SMITH ASKED ABOUT IS, WHY IS
HIS WIFE AN ANTIQUE ADDICT, AN ADDICT ABOUT ANTIQUES?
WHAT YOU THINK ABOUT THAT…WHY IS HIS WIFE AN ADDICT
ABOUT LAMPS AND ANTIQUES.. ABOUT THE OLD STUFF?*

**She has so little in life. I think that's
what she uses to fill it up.**

K. ..WHAT- WHAT IS THE BEST WAY..TO GET HER OUT OF THIS?

Buy her a house   *(little laugh) ..*

OKAY, HYM..

*I think she needs to become more of a person,
  to herself.
She needs to feel she has control of her own life,
 and then she can abandon the props, the junk ,
 the objects. She's using the objects to make up
 a version of reality for herself, you know,
 like making a puzzle.*

*ARE THERE SOME THINGS THAT YOU WOULD LIKE TO SAY TO
   THE SMITH AT THE OTHER END OF THE WELL?*

ANYTHING IN PARTICULAR?

it would be nice to be, ..all together.. / ..altogether.

ANY THOUGHTS TO HIM TO HELP THAT, WHAT TO DO,
TO HELP THAT ALTOGETHER, THE ALTOGETHER-NESS?

it has to be a way to have one belong to the other,
maybe with, maybe with some kind of social
interaction um where you feel more a part
of a c o m m u n i t y.

SO HIS RELATIONSHIP WITH MARTIAL ARTS, PHYSIOLOGY, BODY,
MIND, HIS RELATIONSHIP WITH THE COMMUNITY BEING
A PART OF IT, HELP IN HIS RELATIONSHIP TO THE INNER ..CORE
OF THE WELL?

the problem is just one of communication, I don't
know, there are thes(e) thing(s) holding it back.

SO SOMETHING'S HOLDING IT BACK, THAT COMMUNICATION, AND
WHAT IS THIS THING?

I think there's a lot of, a lot of fear.
there's a lot of sadness. [58]

AND WHAT DOES THAT DO TO...........?

what does that do to who ?   *(Paying Attention!)*

WHAT'S THE REASON FOR THAT FEAR AND SADNESS?

I just think there's too much suffering going on and ..

---

[58] *I'd forgotten all about this part. Although 16 years ago, still I'm surprised*
at my forgetting. Perhaps I was in the well too.   *4-20-2005*

SUFFERING THAT'S NOT ACKNOWLEDGED OR TALKED ABOUT?

well there's a lot of things happening. I've s e e n a lot of things.

TOO MUCH SUFFERING IN THE WORLD? -YOU'VE SEEN A LOT OF THINGS, A LOT OF SUFFERING..

there doesn't seem to be any way to do anything about it.

IS THERE A WAY TO DO ANYTHING OR HELP SMITH THE YOU AT THE BOTTOM OF THE WELL ? IS THERE A YOU, AT THE TOP OF THE WELL? .... IS THERE A SMITH AT THE TOP OF THE WELL?

I don't know. sort of feels like it, but there could be another one. yeah.

WOULD YOU BE OPEN TO, EVERY SO OFTEN, LOOKING UP TOWARDS THE TOP OF THE WELL TO SEE IF THERE'S ANOTHER SMITH, LOOKING DOWN? - - WOULD(N'T) THAT BE, AGREEABLE TO YOU?

I don't know.

SO YOU'RE JUST NOT SURE, YOU DON'T KNOW.

yes

OKAY. ANY OBJECTIONS TO THAT?

no.

OK what about letting yourself float ...
WOULD YOU BE WILLING TO..TALK AGAIN..IN THE FUTURE?

(~)

OKAY THANK YOU.

158

And just letting yourself float now, continue floating, comfortably, letting yourself be ,, noticing that circular staircase, and you will see one of the banisters, you see both banisters, and the up banister ..

and by the time you get to 8 you will feel very energized, and together, *and relaxed,*

1 2 3 4 5 6 7 8 // 3, 2, 1

~

CB: How are you feeling?

Smith: Um, I can barely see. (laugh) - - my arm .. just sore.

CB: ..relaxing it- - any thoughts on this whole experience? What it was like, what it is like?

S: I'm not sure I want to do it <u>again</u>.   *(little laugh)*

CB: why? / *S: well I'm not sure, it seemed like something* was *working. but I don't know what.*

CB: you're not sure you'd want to do it again..? .. because I know what your thoughts are about all this, hypnosis-stuff. Well you say it did feel like something was working?

Smith: Yeah I felt like something was working.

CB: you sure got a lot- a lot of answers. and questions. how did you feel like it was working?

S: well I've never really been in a state of med- meditation or anything like <u>that</u>, so.. I mean I could tell it was deeper than anything like that.

C: yeah..you've never been in that meditation-type stuff?

S: well I've done meditation, but..

CB: oh you have done it, oh okay.. so this was different..

Smith: yeah!

❖

The Third Wave

" For it is exceedingly close to you

in your mouth and in your heart,

that you may do it. "

The Third Wave

Discovery

Think

Recalling, getting into, my inner core,

it seemed like a real peaceful state.

<9>

Estefania

Happiness

May 31st, 1989

.. think back ..

Name	Age	Occupation	Inner contact	Prior therapy
Estefania	45	Travel	5-31-89	27 months

*E*stefanía was refined, a sweet and cultured woman enormously committed to others.

She enjoyed people but Estefanía was upset by intimidation at work and in personal life.

There was intense emotional reactivity to these pressures.

Estefanía was averse to looking into her past, in particular, childhood. Her ideas vis~à~vis´ her Inner core's is noteworthy.

~

Three weeks earlier, Estefanía's son, Jonathan, had reached his Inner core. She saw in amazement the initial development of her son's metamorphosis, his dazzling response. She wanted to reach her own inner core.

~

The Inner highlights Estefanía's lack of contact to her core without explanation as to why, then provides two methods to reach her inner core--one present, one past.

May 31, 1989

CB: I guess I'm organized here...getting these papers,

E: Ahhm

C: Okay so you start by resting the arms comfortably on the couch there, what these arm pillows.. -is that okay?- / *E:* um hym / ..close okay, feel okay?

..because it's for a different purpose, just for comfort rather than for balance, to ..and umm .. *just kind of getting the arms set there (easily, quickly) and then at "one"... looking towards the top of your eyebrows and the top of your head and "1" taking a deep breath ..*

"8" down to "7," 10 times more relaxed, finding that staircase, it may have a comfortable color, carpeting....that you see.. see any particular color? / E: dark blue

.. a very <u>comfortable</u> staircase, with at least one solid banister that you see, that goes down...you're looking down at the staircase at this point...breathing in relaxation...and concentration...and breathing it throughout the body and..

Breathing in, concentration and relaxation and nurturance and then breathing it out .. throughout the being. and with each breath in, and with each breath out, becoming more and more relaxed and comfortable .. and relaxed and comfortable

Perhaps you'd like to know what level of trance you happen to be at.. I'll count to three, and say the word "State," and a number from one to 100 will come to mind, 50 being average or the middle, a hundred being the deepest you can imagine, and one being the lightest.. "1,2,3, State."

E: **50**

okay..just letting yourself Be, on that staircase, and now in looking at that staircase.. you can realize it's not a straight staircase but a circular staircase. And so you can imagine you will be going down that circular staircase. And when you get to the center of the circular staircase, that is when we will be in touch with.. the Inner, the inner..

And now going down that staircase, 6 to 5 becoming ten times more relaxed..is comfortable dark blue staircase..and now you can notice there are really two bannisters, one on either side of the staircase, one banister going down and one coming up..

you notice the one going down .. and you're continuing to float comfortably down "5" down to "4", 10 times more relaxed and down to "3" ..checking the level of trance .. "State!"

E: **3**

Okay.. going deeper and deeper and we get to zero we'll get to the Inner..will be talking with the inner. Breathing in relaxation as you're floating .. the arm will be getting heavier..

"2" going down and let it go... one going deeper floating floating and zero. I'd like to talk to the Inner. Let me know when the <u>Inner</u> is there..

2-3 seconds

Uh hym. *(!)*   *Softly & Emphatically*

DO YOU HAVE A NAME?

Estefanía

OKAY, AND HOW LONG HAVE YOU BEEN AROUND?

40 years   *(or 44)*

AND HAS THE OUTER ESTEFANÍA KNOWN ABOUT YOU?

uh hymm

DO YOU COMMUNICATE WITH HER?

I try to

DOES SHE HEAR YOU ALL THE TIME?

uh hymm

.. SO YOU TRY ..

SOMETIMES YOU CAN GET THROUGH TO HER..?

mostly not

BUT SHE KNOWS ABOUT YOU..

uh hymm

AND YOU KNOW ABOUT HER..

uh hymm

*W<small>HY DO YOU THINK YOU CAN MOSTLY NOT GET THROUGH TO HER,
AND MOSTLY THAT SHE DOESN'T LISTEN TO?..</small>*

I have no explanation for that.

S<small>O YOU KNOW YOU CAN COMMUNICATE AND DO</small> **uh hymm**
*B<small>UT HER HEARING YOU, IN RESPONDING TO YOU, YOU HAVE NO
EXPLANATION FOR WHY, WHY IT DOESN'T HAPPEN MOSTLY ..</small>*

uh hymm

A<small>RE YOU AWARE OF THE QUESTION SHE HAS FOR YOU..TODAY?</small>

slightly

*O<small>NE OF HER QUESTIONS IS ON..ISSUES ABOUT HER INNER HAPPINESS,
AND HER STRUGGLES THAT SHE'S BEEN IN ABOUT THAT.
AND SHE WANTS TO KNOW MORE, ABOUT BEING HAPPY..</small>*

uh hymm *..<small>AND WHAT THAT'S ALL ABOUT.</small>* **uh hymm** ..
*C<small>AN YOU... TELL HER SOMETHING ABOUT THAT? OR SAY
SOMETHING ABOUT THAT?</small>* **uh hymm..**
O<small>KAY WHAT DO YOU THINK ABOUT THAT?</small>

Happiness comes from making yourself happy..
before making someone else happy.

*<small>SO THAT'S THE ESSENCE... OF MAKING YOURSELF HAPPY FIRST..
BEFORE MAKING SOMEONE ELSE HAPPY.</small>* **uh hymm.**
*N<small>OW SHE WANTS TO KNOW ABOUT..NOT NEEDING A RELATIONSHIP,
BEFORE MAKING HERSELF HAPPY..</small>*

uh hymm

C<small>AN YOU SAY SOMETHING ABOUT THAT?</small>

You can be happy with someone .. but they
can't make you happy.

Y<small>OU CAN BE HAPPY WITH SOMEONE</small>~ **right ..**
(<small>TOGETHER</small>~) **.. but they can't make you happy.**

Yes

OKAY .. NOW CAN SHE ASK YOU MORE ABOUT THIS?

uh hymm

HOW CAN SHE DO THAT ... HOW CAN SHE ASK YOU ABOUT THIS?

By meditating

OKAY..BY MEDITATING   uh hymm   *SHE CAN TUNE IN*
uh hymm   *TO YOU*   uh hymm

ANYTHING SHE SHOULD DO WHILE MEDITATING?

Find a quiet place ..without any outside influence..
of sounds.

SO FIND A QUIET PLACE, WITHOUT ANY INFLUENCE OF SOUNDS..

WILL SHE KNOW HOW TO, CONTACT YOU?

10 seconds

no

CAN YOU GIVE HER ANY IDEAS ABOUT THAT..,

WOULD SHE WANT TO KNOW HOW TO .. CONTACT YOU?

yes

OKAY..WHAT ARE SOME IDEAS AS TO HOW SHE COULD CONTACT YOU?
I THINK I SHOULD ASK FIRST, IS IT OKAY WITH YOU,
IF SHE DOES CONTACT YOU?

yes   *Very quietly*

SO HOW ___ SPECIFICALLY SHOULD SHE CONTACT YOU, IN ADDITION
TO MEDITATING IN A QUIET PLACE?

think of herself as she was a young girl.

SO TO THINK OF HERSELF AS A YOUNG GIRL..

DOES SHE HAVE TO DO MORE? .. TO DO NEXT ~ ?

yes.

Remember what it was like..as a young girl,
and hearing the sounds around her.

(Repeating)

Remember what it was like..as a young girl,
and hearing the sounds around her.

.. RIGHT, UH HYMM.

OKAY.. NEXT, IS THERE ANOTHER STEP?

it's difficult. (!)

SO THOSE ARE THE FIRST STEPS ..

ah hymm

TO MEDITATE, THINK ABOUT HERSELF AS A YOUNG GIRL, ..TUNE IN
TO THE SOUNDS..THE FEELINGS?   THERE MAY BE SOME OTHER
STEPS BUT FOR NOW..WE'LL ASSUME THAT WE'LL GET TO THOSE
AT SOME POINT..

uh hymm (!)

WELL SHE HAS SOME QUESTIONS. GOT THAT SOME OF THE
QUESTIONS ABOUT, THE KIND OF WORK THAT SHE WANTS TO DO
OR SHOULD BE DOING. SOME THOUGHTS OR THOUGHTS ON
THE WORK THAT SHE SHOULD BE DOING?

uh hymm

OKAY.. WHAT, WHAT KIND OF WORK, SHOULD SHE BE DOING?

work that's mostly outdoors.

SO, OUTDOOR ENVIRONMENT? THAT WOULD BE GOOD FOR HER?

uh hymm

WHY WOULD IT BE, GOOD FOR HER?

because..she would be happiest in that environment.

AND THAT WOULD BE GOOD FOR HER. ?   *uh hymm*

OKAY..SO TO OUTDOOR WORK **uh hymm** *IS THERE MORE THAT YOU WANT TO SAY ABOUT .. THE WORK?*

it might be service-oriented.

HOW DO YOU THINK SHE FEELS ABOUT HER WORK RIGHT NOW?

it's a job.

WELL JUST A JOB ..

uh hymm

WHAT MIGHT BE MORE HELPFUL TO HER..GOOD FOR HER..SERVICE-ORIENTED? **uh hymm** *AND OUT OF DOORS..* **uh hymm**

DO YOU HAVE ANY IDEA OF WHAT OTHER KINDS OF QUESTIONS, SHE MIGHT HAVE FOR YOU .. ABOUT WORK?

Yes.

does it pay well ? (Small Laugh)

OKAY.. SO THAT'S WHAT SHE WOULD, WANT TO KNOW,

right.

AND YOU'RE LAUGHING ABOUT THAT.

right

HOW DO YOU FEEL ABOUT IT?

.. that's (what's) important.
Do not forget that.

OKAY .. THAT, PAYING WELL IS IMPORTANT.

yes

SHE MIGHT FORGET THAT?

right

SO SERVICE-ORIENTED STILL NEEDS TO PAY.

uh hymm

WHY IS IT IMPORTANT?

Because that's the way she'd be happy, and survive

OKAY.

and be independent.   (Quietly ... couldn't hear this
                                              except with earphones)

SO THAT'S IMPORTANT..

'K, PERHAPS A BIT MORE ON THE RELATIONSHIP OF YOU WITH HER..

   .. SAID THERE IS SOME COMMUNICATION THERE, BUT SHE
       MOSTLY DOESN'T LISTEN.. TO WHERE YOU'RE AT

   uh hymm.

YOU'RE NOT SURE WHY..

   uh hymm

DO YOU HAVE ANY IDEAS ON POSSIBILITIES WHY... WHY NOT ..

   fear of failure

OH!, FEAR OF FAILURE.

   uh hymm

SO IF SHE REALLY LISTENS TO YOU uh hymm , WHAT WILL
       HAPPEN THAT SHE HAS THAT FEAR OF FAILURE?

WHAT DOES SHE THINK?

   That someone else is smarter.
              Street smart.

DOES THIS MEAN SOMETHING ABOUT HER TUNING OUTSIDE,
          uh hymm   RATHER THAN INSIDE?
   uh hymm, right.

173

SO IF SHE TUNES OUTSIDE, SHE'LL SEE THE STREET SMARTS.

right

SO..DO YOU HAVE STREET SMARTS?

n o

YOU DON'T?

uh uhh

BECAUSE THE FIRST THING YOU SAID WAS .. DOES IT PAY WELL?
WHAT (SHE) THINKS, AND THAT'S WHAT YOU THINK.
SOUNDS PRETTY ..SMART.

yeah but not street smart

K., SO IT..DOES SHE HAVE STREET SMARTS, IN TERMS OF THE
OUTER, ESTEFANÍA?

umm just learning

SO SHE NEEDS THOSE..?

uh hymm

AND YOU HAVE.. OTHER SMARTS..

uh hymm

WHAT .. WHAT KIND OF SMARTS DO YOU HAVE?

That .. my brain is not for rent.

OKAY

.. and people won't use it - won't let ..
them use it .. for their advantage.

SO THAT YOU HAVE AND YOU KNOW.

uh hymm

AND IF SHE FORGETS THAT .. **uh hymm**

SHE CAN TURN TO YOU.

uh hymm

'K., WHAT CAN BE DONE FOR NOW AND IN THE FUTURE, FOR HER TO..LISTEN MORE TO YOU?

..ABOUT THOSE SMARTS, THOSE INNER SMARTS?

keep going... to reach to the... to the inside.

WHAT ABOUT THE OTHER WAY AROUND AS WELL?

(checking again)

HOW DO YOU FEEL - MORE REACHING TOWARDS HER?

it's a little bit scary. And a lot of responsibility.

SO A LITTLE SCARY, AND A LOT OF RESPONSIBILITY.

uh hymm

UMM, THE RIGHT AMOUNT OF RESPONSIBILITY, TOO MUCH, TOO LITTLE? WHAT TYPE OF RESPONSIBILITY?

too much responsibility,

TOO MUCH

uh hymm

AND YOU REALLY .. SHE NEEDS, TO REACH TOWARDS YOU. DOES THAT FEEL MORE, MORE CORRECT?

ARE THERE TIMES..GIVEN THAT SHE NEEDS TO REACH TOWARDS YOU, WOULD THERE BE TIMES,..TO KIND OF..REMIND HER YOU'RE THERE, IF SHE WANTS TO?

uh hymm / *OKAY*

HOW WOULD THAT WORK?

Probably at n~i~g~h~t, before she goes to sleep, reviewing the day and checking out.

'K. IS THERE ANYTHING ELSE THAT YOU WANT TO GET THROUGH..TO HER?

8 seconds

I~ she needs one of these meters where you put coins in, as a way of reaching me. (Little laugh) ..

OKAY (little laugh too)   /   (**A happy look**) ..

...THAT YOUR, THAT THE <u>METER IS RUNNING</u>.   (**Laugh**!)

.. JUST - PUT THE COIN IN .. AND.

that's right.   (Mutual laughter)

SO YOU.. <u>YOU WOULD BE THERE</u> ..

Uh hymm (!)   (So sweetly)

.. BUT SHE WOULD HAVE TO PUT THE COIN IN?

Right.

.. IF I'M READING..I'M HEARING YOU RIGHT?

Uh hymm

K.,.. WOULD IT BE OKAY IF WE TALK AGAIN..PERHAPS?

uh hymm

WELL THANK YOU.

uh hymm

(Total Time 20 minutes)

Feel yourself float comfortably floating, deeply relaxing,

floating .. being. Now finding that circular staircase, again and finding that up banister which goes up, ...

And we'll be going up from "0" to "1", and bringing all that relaxation, all that learning, comes back with you if you wish, "2" by the time you get to eight you'll feel very comfortable, relaxed, together, and energized, while being relaxed as well.

176

And "3" coming up, and 4 5 6 7 and 8 and "three" with your eyes closed.. __ and if you wish, you can make a fist with the hand that is down or up, and it may want to come up, and "two" looking up and taking a deep breath, and "one" with the eyes come open and focus back__ and sensation and control returns where you want to be.

C: And how are you feeling?

E: I want you to know, I took an elevator back up.

C: Oh .. save the energy!   *(mutual laughing)*

E: yeah and and,   *(laughing)*

C: So it's a direct way up.

So how are you feeling?

E: Good, uh hymm... This idea of the meter running, that's interesting, and the idea of putting these coins in,

Because I was rejecting everything about going inside of myself, and facing up to it. And why this meter seemed to appear about putting these coins in it.. was sort of interesting.[59]

C: ..well it makes a lot of sense to me. In terms of what I hear from working with other people's core, she's saying or he's saying _ or it's saying, "I'm here for you, _and it's up to you to find the meter or the button, and in this case it's the meter and the coin."

C: Do you remember the statement to make sure the job pays well? / E: yeah / Money is an issue.

E: ...it is. It really is.

---

[59] *"..rejecting everything about going inside of myself, and facing up to it."*
A certain reluctance plagues persons who are averse to reflecting,
to looking inward or backward in time.   *2-6-07*

C: so how you feeling right now?

E: good um hymm

C: Anything else..?

E: Yes. I find it *really interesting* to do this. Uh hymm, I've done something a while ago in terms of .. doing some focusing, and being in contact with big, with the little girl within me.

And in recall of getting into, my inner *core* it seemed like a real peaceful state.

For me having been young, a little girl I remember hearing a plane overhead, getting into the sound of it, the intrigue or the mystery about it.

And being out there in nature, an incredible experience for me. I kind of miss that right now.

I don't..I *do* enjoy the challenge of paperwork umm, and of business and finance and such, but the center of being happy.. being outdoors.. If I could incorporate that in some way..

C: The center of you sounds different than being the little girl umm, though that was a way in. / *E:* uh hymm

C: umm, but the center seems older, and in fact said she was older, I couldn't quite get it. She said she was 40 or-

E: uh hymm

C: So any more thoughts on that, can you describe what it was like, do you know?

E: It feels easier for me to get to, because there done that before, but I feel a lot better, I feel more *present*.. than in the past. In the past it was a sense of *relaxing* where here I feel *stronger*.

C: So it's tuning into a powerful place /*E:* Right/ or stronger place..

E: I feel it sort of humorous too *(Laughing)* that I would charge myself, coins. *(Mutual laughing)*

C: Therapy time.

E: Sure, don't run out of quarters. *(mutual laughing)*

C: Get a whole stack, it's like doing the laundry, even more so.

E: It's true.

C: So you remember that statement about mostly you *don't* listen to her..to it.

E: Mostly not turning to in myself, for answers.
I look outward for answers instead.

.. accepting not only consequences, but confidence in myself.

C: The Inner agreed with that in terms of turning outward for Street smarts, but turning inward for..other Smarts.
I couldn't have said it any better *(Mutual laughter)* ..
well maybe close *(Laughing)* but not to *that* extent.

..I mean if I needed a therapeutic consultation couldn't think of a better therapist around!

(that is, the Inner core)

Estefanía attained solid emotional foundation and a stronger backbone for taking action. She experienced an enjoyable peacefulness, and an increase in strength.

She migrated to another country with her young children-- accepting an offer of work there in research anthropology.

Her new vocation was outdoors and it paid well.

Trust

That was me.

<10>

Anna Bella

Where The Heart Is

June 1st, 1989

Was it the Innermost or an Inner ?

Name	Age	Occupation	Inner contact	Prior therapy
Anna Bella	31	Administrator	6-1-89	14 months

Anna Bella was ingenious, expert at formulating ideas
but not taking them to heart.

Quick, creative and vibrant, Anna Bella was adroit at query
and inquiry, at times possessing gifted insights.

Recovering from a broken relationship, Anna felt insecure
and emotional, and sensed she needed renewed grounding.

After fourteen months of therapy: as we reached this Inner
awareness, responses came with ease, clarity and a plentiful
specificity. It pinpointed Anna Bella's concerns, and trouble in
her connecting with her core.

Afterwards, Anna Bella alternately accepted and rejected,
challenged or appreciated the veracity of her Inner core.

Ultimately she found better emotional security, established
a more meaningful personal relationship, and continued to be
highly effective with her work.

~

Anna Bella has excellent hypnotic abilities, and utilized
these as a coping mechanism for exquisite emotional
protection since early childhood.

Inside much was secret.

We keep it that way. [60]

---

[60] *What follows is a small portion.*   *8-23-2010*

June 1, 1989

. . .

AND ..H<u>O</u>W OR W<u>HY</u> WOULD SHE BE HURT? ..OR GET HURT?

she's too sensitive

SO THAT OUTER ANN..A<u>NN</u>ABELLA IS V<u>E</u>RY SENSITIVE
...TOO SENSITIVE.

hym-hym

AND HOW ARE Y<u>O</u>U WITH SENSITIVITY?

8 seconds

n<u>o</u>t as sensitive

SO YOU..WOULD HANDLE IT DIFFERENTLY..
DO HANDLE IT DIFFERENTLY.

COULD SHE L<u>EA</u>RN SOMETHING FROM YOU ON THIS? ..
IF SHE WERE.. <u>I</u>F SHE WERE .. COMMUNICATING WITH YOU
OR YOU WITH HER? [61]

I.. don't deal with the outside world so I don't have to be sensitive or not sensitive

'_K [62]

She.. has to deal with the outside world

---

[61] *In one way, this* IF *is a test. Would the Inner Voice comply with what might be considered an attempt to introduce something new? ...*

[62] *Response. It holds to its own flexibility, sensibility & reality ~ this is fully in sync with all the Inner core responses.*   *8-23-2010*

183

SO IT'S NOT AN ISSUE FOR YOU. YOU'RE SOLID.[63] YOU'RE IN THERE
AND YOU'RE SOLID AND..YOU DON'T DO WITH THE OUTSIDE WORLD.

hym-hym

..SHE HAS TO DEAL WITH THAT.

hym-hym

COULD SHE DEAL WITH IT EASIER KNOWING ABOUT YOU?

5 seconds

maybe

IT- A POSSIBILITY..

. . .

MAY I ASK YOU ONE .. OTHER THING.., WHERE YOU ARE? IS
THE INNER WHERE YOU USUALLY ARE? .. ARE YOU
IN THE BOTTOM .. ?

uh-huhm

WHERE..   ANY..PARTICULAR PLACE?

7 seconds

near where the heart is ,

OK.   inside.

OKAY   ...   WELL THANK YOU

~

---

[63] *About being* solid, *it was just last week I researched the inner core .. of
the earth, as a metaphor for consciousness. It is solid.*   5-7-2005

184

Two weeks hence,[64] Anna came back with a thought or belief,

"I think that I've come to conc- the conclusion that..
    th-that *I* was talking to you .. last week.

"I mean, I don't *know* for sure." [65]

"Was this me or not me or both?"

Who knows for sure. That awareness may come with time, intention and self-investigation, understanding the overall picture as it unfolds with Self and others. [66]

"Was this my imagination and~or something real?"

Those finding it Inside, may believe what they feel and see, and~or they may not.

"Real" in the minds of many is clarified only after it manifests in or is embraced by the outside world of culture.

Meanwhile or instead, what or whom do you trust the most?
    & who should you trust?

---

[64] *.. I preferred two days to a week for Anna to come back and metabolize this. During those two weeks, Anna received various interpretations, trusting less in her own? A sensitive time for her. Protection of one's own thoughts is key.*
[65] *The Core had provided useful, previously unknown and unknowable data and conceptualization.* Anna Bella continued to grapple with the inner core, as a concept, and what it may or may not mean for her inner life.   *8-19-2010*
[66] *None of those in this book were privy to any others' experiences until now.*

Find

Instead of an out-of-body experience

I had an inner-body experience.

<11>

Armondo

June 6th, 1989

That's a Perception.

Name	Age	Occupation	Inner contact	Prior therapy
Armondo	38	Postal	6-06-89	19 months

*A*rmondo spoke without hesitation
and with no silences.

His first pause here is in five pages.

This will demonstrate a contrast between the outer person and the inner core. The outer voice does not stop. The Inner voice does not keep going.

The Inner is concentrated, unhurried, soothing, unrushed. It integrates details and the overview, the *"trees"* with *"forest,"* and evidently weds thought with emotion.

~

Armondo was in post-therapy for growth and development. He completed an intensive therapy, having worked through his suffering from the breakup of a seven-year relationship.

One question never fully asked, remained, *"Now what?"*

In discussing our doing core work, Armondo mentioned he had always felt a part of his *mother* with him. He hadn't seen her in years but thought she was always there, watching over him.

In hypnosis, inquiry about this provided him an answer.

~

After a year of standard therapy, we continued to meet though infrequently. Armondo discussed his life over the past six months, *"Things going pretty well, with maybe some mild downs, some mild depression...then things going right back up, going along, with some concerns."*

Armondo agreed to take another step forward, to attempt reaching in hypnosis something called an Inner core.

Armondo thinks he may understand the idea a little bit.

He mentions he might have a guardian angel--his mother!

It will take some time in our session to begin our search for the inner core. The preliminaries provide a flavor of who one is on the inside of the Outer, in comparison with who one is on the outside of the Inner.

June 6, 1989

CB: ...useful thing using hypnosis, using it more fully, so it's been really.. tremendous..

A: oh, I see.   *CB:* ...interesting things have come from it.

CB: so I'm doing a lot of taping. .. so I'll tell you more about it and see what you think..

A: oh OK-how's your friend? the one recuperating from uh..

CB: oh..surgery?

A: Surgery, yeah.

CB: She's just about fully recovered..she forgets sometimes that she still has a little you know, recovery to *do*.. she's back picking things up and..

A: ...she had back surgery?

CB: no, female surgery...around the stomach area.

A: Yeah *(loud cough)* those are hard! / *CB:* yeah.

A: Oh I went through a period of those too, with ah, with Barbara. So they do forget, they want to get up. Actually they do encourage you to start getting up and .. walk around.

CB: oh, yeah! but she sat up in the middle of surgery and said, "Hey it's cold here. I need a blanket."

A: Bet *that* scared them. / *CB:* yeah.. *(laughing loudly)*

A: ...But, anyway, that league that they canceled, because not very many people were showing up. So.. /*CB:* yeah./ ...so I'm waiting for, to see what happens for lone volleyball in Oak Park on Wednesday nights...so are you open on Wednesdays?

{ ...*Continuing* ...on volleyball... basketball...}

CB: Well..what's been happening? It's been about a month.

A: Yeah *(sniff in)* Not much..you know, been pretty low-key. And uh.. I am just finding out..and actually after 38 years, I'm finding out that, you know like uh, that the, the ..

(..a bit loudly, nonstop throughout..)
..mood swings that we all have, you know..

CB: ...the peaks and valleys...?

A: Yeah, the peaks and valleys and the things that happen in your life. You know if you happen to be in a good mood, and something down happens to you.. you can pick it up more... and and and, feel better about it you know. So..

CB: You're making the sign of a *wave*..

A: yeah.

CB: So..so when you're down, you know that you'll be coming back up.. ?

A: Yeah! Well you know, like, so, so you know, I'm I'm learning, I'm learnt, to have a lot more patience. It's you know, I, my feelings, it's like.. Now all of a sudden, I think *(sniff in)* I think I got myself pretty much together. You know.

So now it's like, you know um I don't want to be by myself now anymore, you know what I mean? So now I got to know me so now..an' an' you know..? I'm starting to-

CB: ..you're getting out again..

A: I'm starting to have these yearnings to you kno' have, have somebody else in my life.

And you know, and I, you know, in a way, you know, I don't.. I don't like to operate by myself. I always like to have somebody, because I have that little motivation you know to have somebody else, you know like my house..is, I don't work on it as much as I like to, because I- you know..I don't have a motivation more or less. You know, I mean it takes a little more.. So, that's, you know, that's about it.

CB: That's your.. it's been quite..a long journey.. //

A: yeah! Very long, you know I feel- //

CB: ..Part of the journey for the past year and a hal- //

A: -almost two years, right? //

CB: ..two years? more than a year-and-a-half .. //

A: I started in November 1987.. //

CB: yeah.. so that's a little over, a year and a half, and then a year we were working together about every other week, and the last six months it's been about once per month.. /A: yeah / ..sometimes, every two months.

And..you're moving from.. really taking a look at yourself.. and decon- deconnecting with Barbara to ah.. being more with yourself.. building your own house, really- //

A: yeah kind of like, you know- //

CB: -and now moving beyond *that*-.. //

A: I look like I force myself to .. myself, finally, you know force myself to y'kno *learn* and- *(sniff)* I mean, it's still, there's a lot of things y'kno that I, you know. I guess we're always improving. We're never satisfied as far as y'know- //

CB: Well. I-

A: -where all of a sudden one little problem replaces another one, once- / *C:* yeah,- / if it wants to do that, life- I guess life is like that..

..all the time, y' know you're not gonna- stop- y'know, I I ..always thought that ,, ..you know for a long time it was like, I didn't have that much problem that many problems in in life and everything. Y'know. It's just that maybe I just didn't pay attention to the problems when they would come up. And now I'm forced to, you know, / *C:* .. to.. / face the problems-

CB: ...to pay more attention. -Well you know, the thing I mentioned earlier.. ah re<u>a</u>lly just since we've last met it's become even m<u>o</u>re clear. I may have mentioned it though the last time we met but it's only been the last..two months. /um hymm/ It's really been an experience..of tuning in to the inside, of the person. And we get like.. any questions you want.. to know.. ah you get an<u>s</u>wered basically. Um-/

A: By *yourself* you mean? / yeah! / um- / um *(little sniff)* /

CB: It's like..going to a therapist who's ahh..just knows you inside and out. Because, *(laugh)* it *is* you!- /*A:* ah huh, yeah!-/ So, a therapist can know you pretty well.. and get to know you and..do the best he can../ *(talking the same time)* / *(continuing)* .. related to you as a separate human being, and I sh<u>ou</u>ld be. /*A:*um huh../ Ah..I knew one, one person who'd say, "I know you like a book." His name was Allan Bloom, "I know you like a book, .. "but we're only on chapter 1." (*A: laughing*) I used to resent that (*A: laughing*), "Why should <u>he</u> know me like a book when <u>I</u> don't know me like a book?"

A: Right, yeah. *(laughing)* But it's a lot easier for *you* to know. Because, because you're..you're more objective than I would be.

CB: Some things I might see, and other things ah- // well-

A: -well I don't know, it's easier, y'kno that's why I cherish, my friends' opinion, you know not that I act on them all the time, / *C:*..yeah.. / and and and uh-/ *C:* Well-

CB: -well, how would you feel if you could get that same thing, even more so from your *self* as well? Or primarily?

A: (quietly) Well..I guess it would be good, I don't know,,/

CB: So if you'd like to do that we can *do* that.

A: (quietly) ,, well, what what what do you do..?

CB: Uh first I talk to you about.. uh what you want to know, or what your concerns are / *A:* uh huh /.. about your life. And um, I'll write them down.. on the paper here.. And then, go in to hypnosis, and get in touch with, with the *Inner* / *A:* um hymm/ ..um, and um..see.. what the response is..

So there's really two things..

It's, establishing a relationship you may or may not already have.. with with the Inner. /*A:* uh huh/ Um or developing that, that relationship the way you want it to be.

..as well as asking any questions you know, that you, getting anything across / *A:* um huh / .. that you'd like to get *across.*

(*First silence ~ 1.5 secs*)

So does that ah .. does that make sense?

A: (quietly) Yeah it does, I guess so, yeah, y'know.. I guess we could try it..I y'know, I guess I can't, I can't lose anything by not.. *(slurred)* (if) *not* there. /

CB: Yeah it's, it's uh..we've done some hypnosis before .. but we haven't done this. / *A:* Uh-huh..

CB: It's really been..been ah.. -I have to smile when I say it- because I- The last couple of months it's been really.. *interesting..* /*A:* uh huh/ ..to say the least.

So.

A: Is that the same hypnosis we did before? is-

CB: Well it uses the same idea / *A:* uh huh / .. the same *approach* but it gets more into the.. *(quietly)* the Inner.

Uhh.. So..   [quietly - setting up]

18 secs

CB: Looking at the last- since we've met over the last six months, it's been like, things have been going 'pretty well,' I would consider, maybe some mild 'downs,' you know some mild depression just like you were describing. / yeah / and then going right back up. Things going along /*A: (sniff in)* pretty well..umm.. and um you know, and some concerns-.. //

A: (Louder again) Sometimes I feel like you know, why is, why is the world picking on me? you know, and then the next day well, such a nice day!, y'know. /*CB:* yeah / I had a a.. one of the worst one I had this past month was a .. you know selecting an assistant union steward, I was a running, I was a running mate of a guy that became the union steward. So that..these people were unhappy with him, and ahh *(clears throat),* they were coming and talking to me, *(Picking up speed)* and I said "well, and you know, if you," because he was doing things that looked, and they felt it's not right, like turning your own people *in,* and when you're a union steward you don't turn them in, you know, that's a- an' an' he didn't mean to, he's just tryin' to do good. So I- I kept on saying, you know, "we meet once a month upstairs; you guys come over and *tell* him, I mean talk to him, sit down and talk to him. You elected him, you can tell him what you want from him and expect from him-."

CB:-yeah-

A: So..you know those people just would not talk to him. So the next thing I know I see a petition, you know, you know, from from somebody, which I am not friends with anymore because I .. I .. we started..we were good friends at one time.

CB: So instead of talking to him, they put this whole thing tog- /*A:* yeah/ this peti-

A: yeah, they went behind his back, *(Talking faster)* and they put the petition and they actually voted him out and everything.

194

And I got, I got voted out with him *(breathing out).* And so.. *(Very loudly)* so it's pretty bad, because I felt bad, it was not being voted out, it's just that I felt- // *(Talking together)*

CB: you didn't really *want* to be-

A: NO THAT'S IT and you kno', that didn't, that didn't bother me. But I was just so mad, about, how these people went, you know and all of a sudden..how *powerless* you are because, people you know, people can go ahead and do, whatever they want to *do*, and especially in mass *(talking together).* That meeting left me pretty powerfully, you know powerless. And I was real- you know, I was real pissed. You know and I didn't even call this guy, he was a snake, which I thought was very snaky, you know. It's very underhanded come like that without talking to somebody you know. Now, you know, and eventually he won, you know. And now they're supposed to be the big wheels and everything, you know, and I'm sittin' there and I see these guys are havin' the same problem that I had. You know. And they're doing the same thing that everybody else is doing, you know, no different.

CB: so it's like, um.. /A: *(Loudly)* So that was -

CB: ..a new union steward and things will get better- /

A: ..they're not going to get better, you know.

CB: ..like a scapegoating..

A: ..that's what it was this guy's got a bug up his ass. You know, he caught him and he, he.. he..   *Continuing 2 minutes*

A: {*On political action, meetings, microwaves, union dues, representation, signatures, and..}* ..dragging their feet..you could just tell what they were doing..

CB: Well..do you think what we..will do today.. if you'd like to do that..could respond to some of this?

A: ..Yeah.

CB: So what questions would you like? ..something about the uh..the valleys and the peaks?

A: (Louder) I don't know, y'know I guess the question that's been bugging me, you know, lately is this uh, .. you know, I'm tired of being a nice guy, you know?, because every time I.. you know, I'm in .. every time I get in a situation, especially with a lady, you know, "oh yeah you're a nice man, *but..*" you know. And uh, and I guess I'm not aggressive enough, and so you know, so.. Women feel comfortable, and then you know, when I try to make moves, too late, because they feel so comfortable, you know that they don't wanna do, they don't want to get involved in and or anything, you know, so. I think that's, that's what lately has been bothering me lately as far as that, because I because I-

CB: Is that because they regard you as a human being, instead of.. /*A: (breathes out)* / ..just a sex object?

A: well no it's not- I'm not saying- yeah you know, I mean it's like you know- I'm just tired of this, it gets frustrating, you know I mean like, right now you know I'm ready to start going on trying to meet someone, you know?

And-

CB: -so it's how to meet- ? - *(Talking together: a friendly and continuing battle for structure)* or- //

A: And there's a certain move or approach there..and it's not necessarily a *sexual* move, but a move that, I used to have, and I don't have it anymore, you know I think I'm scared..   *1 minute*

{ *Discussing what kind of move, person-to-person relating working against him?, talking with a woman, being a nice guy, assertiveness...* }

CB: So, ..so it's a nice guy..and it's *assertiveness*! You had mentioned that a *long* time ago.. /*A:* Um-hum/ ..about using hypnosis regarding assertiveness.. um, something like that?..is that..the word? / *A:* yeah.

2+ seconds

CB: 'k.. any, any other, things you like to know or..? How much do feel in touch with the inner part of you, right now?

A: I don't know, I feel, I feel pretty much, you know, pretty well in touch with myself..   *2 seconds*   to..to the point while where I know I I know if I could notice if I'm lying to myself or not..you know..so.

CB: yeah.

A: (clearing throat, breathing out)

CB: .. so how do you *notice* that?

A: I don't know, there's just something insid- a voice inside of me says I. I. you know.. *(talking together)*

CB: yeah-.   *A:* You know.

A: -it's like ok y'kno you, it's like, a little nagging voice in back y'kno'- I think it's like part of my mother[67] stayed with me y' know.

CB: ..sound like mother's voice..? /

A: yeah..No!, no, it's just..got a little guardian angel that.. you'know.

CB: that's there.

A: ..planes have y'know, planes have uh..alarms when they start going too low, or y'know too slow or whatever, so that's what. // *(..talking together..)* //

A: ..I have a little alarm s' *doodle-oodle-oodle-oodle-oodle!*

CB: (w/ Serious chuckle) ..Right!

A: ..which I like that, I like that very much /C: yeah!/ *(More quiet, seriously)* because then it keeps me honest and then I can be honest with other people. / *C:* yeah..

CB: (Animatedly) .. Well do you want to try this?

---

[67] *Armondo was estranged from his mother, who he described in writing as,* " ...a strong woman--that had high hopes for me. Pushy. "

197

A: ...yeah we can try it.

CB: ...and we'll do this. /*A:* hymm?/ *CB:* We can try it and we'll *do* it.

A: okay, so..

CB: um..okay, so..you might want to try this this side..that feel okay ? /*A:* okay/..the 'hypnosis' side of the couch.

A: (Loud laugh)

CB: (laughing together) Not that you h<u>a</u>ve to be there but y'know, it doesn't hurt. And there's the foot- / *A:* Ohh!! / Did we do the foot stool last time?

A: emm I don't think so, I don't remember.

CB: it was a while back. OK...

A: I might fall asleep on you now..   *(Chuckle)*

CB: Okay we'll see how it goes.

A: ..because this is my nap time   *(Laughing)*

CB: Ah, okay you start by getting comfortable as your feet are and then.. -here's some pillows- and your other arm comfortably resting on- *[Microphone falls]*

A: I can hold it.   *(Mutual hearty*

CB: ..but then it would go up like *this*.   *Laughter)*

CB: What I'll do is put it over here, and then when your arm's up, I'll move it back.

A: okay.

CB: So, okay! You start by getting comfortable, want those feet crossed or uncrossed?.. /*A:* does it matter?/ Whatever's comfortable. ..And is the .. Spray propellant *(on his belt)*, is that comfortable?

A: it feels good.

CB: It, it looks like it could be aimed to keep people away y'know, but it is aiming this way..   *(jokingly)*

A: Everybody goes, "Is that for people?," I go, "It is for dogs but," I say, "it does work on people too, remember that."
(Laughing)

CB: OK.. So.. ahh do you remember how it, how it goes?

A: not, not doing..

CB: -it'll come right back to you.

The last time I have down here was, over a year ago..April 26, 1988, is that possible? / *A:* yeah! / Have you been doing much of it yourself or any of it? / *A:* not much, no. *(sounding sleepy)* / Ok so start over here.. / *A:* ok / So you can put your head..

look at, look at me with your head .. right. ummm, then look up towards the top of your eyebrows, now the top of your head, and while looking up..slowly closing your eyelids while taking a deep breath...closing, closing, eyes up..closing.. holding the breath. Now breathing out, relaxing the eyes, floating down and letting the hand float up, while the body floats down.

Going deeper and deeper, more relaxed breathing in relaxation .. breathing in care and nurturence, than breathing it throughout the body, throughout the being..

Breathing in relaxation..and breathing it throughout.. breathing in nourishment and nurturence..going deeper and deeper as your arm goes up..

You can let it go up, if you'd like to imagine a balloon attached to it you can, and you can let it go up, the more it goes up the deeper relaxed..you become and..the more in trance you can go..And you can focus easier and easier on the sound of my voice and let go of any..other..extraneous..sounds that are not of particular interest to you.

But you can find it very easy to ss.. follow the sound, and follow the meaning, of the words, and of the phrases, of what's being said. At the same time, you can let yourself relax and kind of sleep..at the same time focusing clearly and easily on the sound of my voice.

You can notice a staircase, a very comfortable looking staircase with a thick banister, on it. In fact you can notice two banisters, one happens to be a down banister and the other happens to be an up banister.. but in any case you're appreciating the staircase ... and it may have a color, a comfortable looking color on the stairs... on the carpeting, however it's constructed..do you see a color?

And, what color do you see? -

..and you can say it very readily and easily and still maintain, the trance.

(Slowly)

A: " I see a tan color. "

Okay. And you can be going down that staircase, from "8" down to "7," going down the staircase getting 10 times more relaxed, 10 times more relaxed, going deeper.. into a floating, a comfortable floating-down feeling...

And perhaps you would like to know what level trance you're at, whatever that might be from 1 to 100 where the hundred is the deepest you can imagine, and one is the lightest and 50 is right in the middle. So at the count of three I'll say the word "state," and number will pop to mind, and you'll say that number easily and readily, whatever it happens to be. 1,2,3, state!

" 50 "

Okay. And now moving down that staircase very comfortably .. tan staircase ..

..from "7" down to "6" 10 times more relaxed, going to a deeper, relaxed place.. letting go of any uh..tensions or any, specific concerns at the moment; by breathing in the relaxation and the nurturence and then breathing it throughout the body....

You begin to notice that that staircase that you're looking down is really a circular staircase, it's a circle, circular staircase that goes down and down.. And when we get down to the bottom of the center of the cir- circular staircase, we'll be in touch with the Inner!

Now going from "6" down to "5" 10 times more relaxed.. just drifting and relaxing.. You may notice that the, you may or may not notice.. that the arm begins to get somewhat heavier. As it gets heavier, it may start coming back down.. and, becoming even more and more deeply relaxed.. As you're going down the staircase..10 times more relaxing going from the "six" to the "five" to the "4" and "state!"

10 secs

" 70 "   *(very quietly)*

..ok a number comes to mind, 70; 'k, deeply relaxing..."3" 10 times more relaxed arm getting heavier and heavier, moving down, deeper into hypnosis.. "2" going deep and relaxing..

And "1." Many more times relaxed.. Ultimately more, relaxing and, going deeper and down.

And "zero." .. and let me know when the Inner is there ..

~ AND I'D LIKE TO SPEAK WITH THE *INNER.*

10 secs   *Moving microphone..*

He's here

OKAY .. WHAT DO I CALL YOU?

2 secs

Armondo

201

OKAY .. DO YOU HAVE ANY OTHER NAME?

3 secs

uh-em

OKAY .. NOW HAVE YOU.. HOW LONG YOU BEEN..THERE?

3 secs

all my life.

*SO HAVE YOU BEEN WITH THE OUTER ARMONDO/**m-hm***
..ALL HIS LIFE?

m-hym

DO YOU TALK WITH HIM?

m-hym

DOES HE TALK WITH YOU?

m-hym

OKAY. IS HE ALWAYS IN TOUCH WITH YOU?

uh-uh

OH..SOMETIMES, SOMETIMES NOT..

m-hm

OKAY. HOW MUCH IN TOUCH IS HE WITH YOU?

he hasn't been in touch with me for'while.

..FOR HOW LONG?

long time

..YEARS?

m-hm

'K, WHEN DID HE STOP BEING IN TOUCH?

I don't know

BUT IT'S BEEN A LONG TIME. / **m-hm** */ ..FOR YEARS.*

m-hmm

DID ANYTHING HA<u>PP</u>EN, WHERE HE STOPPED BEING IN TOUCH
WITH YOU?

10 secs   *horn sound*

emmmm..   (Deep breath in~out)
he just want to do what he want to do.
SO HE JUST WENT HIS OWN WAY.. ?

m-hmm
'K..
found other things
OTHER THINGS TO DO?

m-hmm
AND HOW DO YOU FEEL OR THINK ABOUT THAT?

4 secs

I'm still here ..

SO IF HE..IF HE WA<u>N</u>TS TO BE IN TOUCH.. YOU, YOU'RE
STILL THERE. YOU'RE..

we've been in touch.

'K. ARE YOU WAITING FOR HIM TO GET BACK IN TOUCH WITH YOU?

he's been getting back in touch.
O'K SO IT'S..IT'S KIND OF UP TO HIM.. **m-hmm**
HOW MUCH HE WANTS TO GET BACK IN TOUCH.. **m-hmm**
AND YOU'RE..YOU'RE THERE. **m-hmm**
AND..HOW LONG WILL YOU BE THERE?

all the time.

OKAY

NOW HE- HE DID HAVE SOME QUESTIONS..OR SOME CONCERNS, ABOUT..HE AND THE WORLD, WHERE ONE DAY HE'LL FEEL.., 'WHY IS THE WORLD PICKING ON ME?' AND THE NEXT DAY HE'LL FEEL BETTER. SO HE- HE'S WONDERING ABOUT THE UPS AND DOWNS.

WHAT DO YOU THINK ABOUT THAT?

5 secs

has to take the good with the bad.

OKAY. WHY DOES THE WORLD SOMETIMES SEEM TO PICK ON HIM?

3 secs

it doesn't pick on him, that's just the way the world is.

OH OKAY..

it's not personal.

..THAT'S JUST THE WORLD, IT'S NOT PERSONAL..

that's..

that's a perception.

SO HE HAS A PERCEPTION THAT THE WORLD IS PICKING ON HIM.

m-hmm

..BUT JUST THE WORLD. WHY DOES HE HAVE THE PERCEPTION.. THAT THE WORLD IS SOMETIMES PICKING ON HIM?

because he's alone I guess.

AHHM.. WOULD HE FEEL LESS ALONE.. HOW, HOW WOULD HE FEEL LESS ALONE?

somebody he can love.

OKAY.. SOMEBODY OUT THERE?

m-hmm

WHAT ABOUT HIS RELATIONSHIP WITH YOU AS WELL?

4 secs

He's.. he.. he's not alone here.

OKAY. SO HE'S NOT ALONE.

m-hm..

YOU..YOU KNOW THAT.

m-hmm.

DOES HE KNOW THAT?

m-hmm.

O-KAY. IT'S JUST A MATTER OF HOW MUCH, HE WANTS TO TUNE IN ..TO YOU **m-hmm** *..AS WELL.*

HE DOES HAVE A CONCERN ABOUT..HOW TO REACH OUT.. (horn) *TO PEOPLE OUT THERE IN THE WORLD.. ESPECIALLY HOW TO DEAL WITH WOMEN. HE SAID HE SOMETIMES IS TIRED OF BEING..THE NICE GUY.*

he cares too much about friendship.

IN..IN WHAT WAY..OR WAYS?

he just dosnt want to hurt anybody.

SO HE CARES TOO MUCH..

...so he doesnt take a chance
and he doesnt wan-to-get-hurt either.

SO HE REALLY PROTECTS HIMSELF AND PROTECTS THE OTHER PERSON. **m-hmm** *..AND DOESN'T TAKE A CHANCE.*

DOES HE KNOW THAT?

m-hmm.

WHAT..WHAT DOES HE NEED TO DO IN TERMS OF..REACHING OUT?

4 secs

not be afraid of getting hurt.

'K AND HOW- HOW DOES HE DO THAT?

take a chance.

'K. DOES HE HAVE TO BE AFRAID OF BEING HURT?

2 secs

uh-uh..

1 sec

no.

WHY DOES HE THINK HE HAS TO BE AFRAID OF BEING HURT?

I dont know.

*BUT YOU KNOW..THAT, HE..DOESN'T HAVE TO FEEL AFRAID
OF BEING HURT..*

no.

'K, .. AND WHY IS THAT?

**because, he might not be hurt..
if you take a chance.**

'K., SO IT'S THAT SIMPLE?

m-hmm.

OK. HE WONDERS IF HE'S SCARED OF COMMITMENT   *(horn)*
..TOO

no.

HE'S NOT SCARED OF COMMITMENT.. ?

no.

OKAY. UMM..HE ALSO MENTIONED THAT HE HEARS A VOICE WHEN HE'S LYING TO HIMSELF

that's me.

OH, OKAY

ARE YOU PART OF HIS MOTHER?

uh-uh. i'm part of him.

OH OKAY.. 'CAUSE HE MENTIONED IT WAS LIKE..A LITTLE GUARDIAN ANGEL..

that's me.

OK.. AND ARE YOU A GUARDIAN ANGEL?

m-hymm.

AND YOU'RE NOT PART OF HIS MOTHER.

uh-uh.

'K. NOW HE FEELS HE'S PRETTY WELL IN TOUCH WITH HIMSELF.. ESPECIALLY ABOUT THE LYING OR NOT. IS HE?

I think so

OK.. THAT HE'S PRETTY WELL IN TOUCH. AT THE SAME TIME YOU SAID HE REALLY HASN'T COMMUNICATED WITH YOU IN YEARS..DIRECTLY.

no. but's been in touch since he's ..(been in) himself.

SO HE'S BEEN IN TOUCH..SINCE HE'S.. **m-hymm** *SINCE HE'S..? WHAT DID YOU SAY?*

been by himself.

BEEN BY HIMSELF. BEEN MORE IN TOUCH WITH YOU? **m-hymm** *..SINCE HE'S BEEN BY HIMSELF. /* **m-hymm**

OK.

WHAT YOU THINK HE NEEDS RIGHT NOW?

9 secs

Somebody in~is~life.

'K.

he likes to s-h-a-r-e.

AND HOW..HOW WILL YOU FEEL ABOUT THAT?

Good.   *GOOD?*   **m-hymm.**

DO YOU SHARE IN THAT TOO?   **m-hymm.**

'K. *CAN YOU HELP HIM ACHIEVE THAT?*

I don't know.

CAN HE TURN TO YOU FOR..FOR HELP WITH THAT?

m-hymm.

'K. *SO IF HE TURNS TO YOU, THAT WOULD, THAT WOULD*
WORK OUT   **m-hymm**   *..FINE.*

IS THERE TIMES, IF IT'S OKAY WITH HIM, THAT YOU CAN
REACH OUT..TOO?   **m-hymm.**

SO THERE ARE TIMES..IT'S OKAY..THAT YOU CAN REACH OUT

i do reach out.

OH YOU DO REACH OUT. WHAT, AT WHAT TIMES?

when he needs me.

OKAY.. DOES HE HAVE TO KNOW THAT AND SAY THAT?

no.

SO EVEN IF..YOU KNOW THAT..IF HE NEEDS YOU..YOU'LL
BE THERE FOR HIM.

m-hymm.

IS THERE ANYTHING YOU' LIKE TO COMMUNICATE TO HIM?
TO THE OUTER ARMONDO..

5 secs

everything's going to be all-right.

OK. IS THERE ANYTHING ELSE RIGHT NOW, THAT HE NEEDS
TO KNOW FROM YOU?   **m-hm,**

that I'm always the̲re.

OKAY. OK. SO..HOW DOES HE HAVE TO...TO DO THINGS..OR
WHAT DOES HE HAVE TO DO TO GET IN TOUCH WITH YOU?

i'm always in there, I know what's going on.

'K. AND HE CAN.. UMM CAN HE FIN-

i let him know.

OKAY. CAN HE FIN- CAN HE FIND YOU EASILY?   **m-hymm.**
AND YOU LET HIM KNOW?

he does find me, he knows how.

OKAY.

WOULD IT BE ANY DIFFERENT FOR HIM TO BE IN CLOSER TOUCH
WITH YOU THAN HE HAS IN RECENT YEARS?

m-hymm

HOW WOULD IT BE?

it'd be.. it c'd be better.   *(a bell)*

'K..   **it is better.**

SO IT I̲S BETTER.. AND IT'D BE..BETTER AND BETTER?

m-hymm.   *OK*

..'K..HOW WAS IT TALKING..RIGHT NOW?

good

209

K. AND..IF YOU'D LIKE, AND HE'D LIKE, AND I'D LIKE,
COULD WE BE..BACK IN TOUCH?

m-hymm.

OKAY. THANK YOU.

Okay, and now just   *(horn sound)*
.. floating and drifting .. and before we go,
WHERE ARE YOU..WHERE ARE YOU LOCATED?

in the heart.

OK. SO YOU..ARE RIGHT IN..IN THE HEART

m-hymm.

AND WHERE IS THAT?

its all over the body.

OK. AT WHAT..WHAT PLACE IS IN THE BODY? IS IT IN THE BODY?

its in the spirit.

OK. AND WHERE IS THAT?

its within/ within Armondo.

OK, IT'S WITHIN..ARMONDO'S SPIRIT?

m-hymm.

NOW IS THAT INSIDE THE BODY?   **m-hymm**.

.. THROUGHOUT..   **m-hymm**.

IS IT EVERYWHERE?

Everywhere.

OK. OKAY WELL THANK YOU..
APPRECIATE IT.

Okay, now just drifting... and floating.. comfortably being wherever you wish to be and need to be.. continuing with the comfortable breathing and the relaxation..

And now finding yourself on that circular staircase..some- where.. You may notice the tan~ness and the..good feeling of that staircase.. Now you may notice that up banister.. (winding) round and up that staircase...up from "zero" to "1" ..bringing back 10 times more energy and relaxation back with you to "2" ..

By the time you get to 4 you'll feel..a.. very enjoyable connection with yourself.. and bringing back a gift, bringing back whatever you wish to bring back..

From "1" to the "2" coming up and then the "3"..and the "4".."5".. feeling very good and energized and relaxed -assertive- and "6".. and "7" very good, and "8"..

Now three getting ready, with your eyes closed, rolling up your eyes, and coming up..and two opening, with your eyes open, making a fist with the hand that is up, and one focusing your eyes and letting your arm move back down.

A: (Big breath in)

Take a deep breath. Let it out. And as you open your hand, your arm.. your usual sensation and control returns.

*Your arm can float down. O*r you can put it down or whatever you want to do with it.

A: (Big wake-up yawn) ..OOhh!

CB: So..!

A: (sniff in)

CB:.. how *was* that?

A: it was pretty good! .. pretty re*lax*ing.

CB: Do you remember *all* of it..some of it?

A: uhhym.

CB: okay. So..it was..relaxing. /*A:*uhhym/ -in want..what way? how was it?

A: *(A quiet wake-up voice:)*

I don't know, just like, you know ..nice and.. *groovy!*

CB: *(Laugh)* ..'cause you said you might fall as*leep!!*

A: *(Loudly with fun)*..No!..yea..so..its..y'kno.. I started dri<u>ft</u>ing .. I got, like really into like..into the stairs. I was like, y'kno, and then, and then.. I was *listening* to you, and then I kind of lost a couple of, you know, things you were saying. And then it was jus like..you know. [68]

CB: ..you came *back.*   *A:* uh-huh.   *CB:* yeah.

4 second pause

A: *(breathes out, clears throat)*

CB: *(breathes in)*

So how..how do you feel now, and..?   *(Musical*

A: .. peppy!   *sounds)*

CB: ..peppy. And *groovy.*

A: yeah, and groovy /   *CB:* *(Laughing)*

CB: Any thoughts you have about, what went on .. ?

A: I don't know, feels *good!* It feels good, to be able to kind of ah express your inner thoughts through- it makes you more aware now..of yourself.

C: So it's a feeling of more, expressing..your inner thoughts right now..out there, yeah.

A: yeah I have a feeling of *awareness* to͘o, y' know.

CB: ..what..what type..?

---

[68] *On Recall Questionnaire Armondo describes, "Stairs, me, fog, warmth" and nothing more.*

A: I don' kno' .. I felt like I was, *inside* y'kno, not as far as physical but as far as y' know, spirit-, spiritual-type y'know, you're inside your body. Instead of having an out-of-body experience, I had like an *inner-body* experience y' know.

CB: yeah! it's, it's, all in-, in-

A: -especially when you go down the stairs. It feels like you're going in some deep..dark..dungeon. And y'know f-m-js-lk-its the stairs like make it real warm so it's not like, y' know..a bad place you're going to. /*CB:* ahhym / ..an *isolated* place, that y'kno'.

CB: Do you think you've been in *touch* with that..that *part* that was in that deep dark.. / *A:* yeah I think so, / ..dungeon?

A: ..I think you know, *part* of it, yeah.

CB: Because I got really two, two feelings one uh yeah that well, you believe you're pretty well in touch with yourself, and the response than I got, 'yeah you're pretty well in touch;' at the same time maybe you haven't communicated for a number of years.. *directly.*

A: (Loudly and Very Quickly..) [69] I think that's a, you know, thas I think a little less of that, y'know, it's like, I kind of drifted, y'know, especially when you..when you're with someone (when you do so) when you're livin' with someone else you're sharin' your life with somebody else, you're kind of like.. you lose your..your, whada-you-call-it.. your uniqueness.. being yourself.

.. because you have to share your life with, sharing your life an', y'know how they say sometimes couples that starten' to look alike because they've been together so long, /*C:* yeah/..so, you lose your self~ness.

CB:.. you lose your *self*..

---

[69] *To be able to hear this, required slow-play many times.*   *4-18-2005*

A: yeah..so that's what I think that's what it was, that I was not in touch with my self. Or ah- Although y'know I'm pretty perceptive, to y'know as far as that.

I mean it's not like I- I wasn't completely in *touch.* It's just that I was not *listening* ..y'know.

CB: yeah.

A: -y'know especially if I would have listened I would have been out of the relationship *way* before. *(yawn)* ..y'know! *(exhale)*

CB: yeah

A: -you know, it *ended.* Way way before. So.

CB: You know in terms of future relationships the secret is if you stay in touch with yourself <u>and</u> have a relationship.

A: The thing y' know in future relationships, the secret is that I have to have, *me-time,* where I never had before. You know I always wanted to do something together and everything, and you need that- y' know whether -'me-time' as far as.. You can be with somebody but .. y'know, you don't have to talk, you don't have to do nothin', you just relax and listen to music and just, you know have your thoughts! Your inner thoughts, whatever think about it and just, don't *share* everything, you know, just keep it to yourself! I think that's, y'know, I need to..to have some of *that. (Wistfully:)* You know I like now my me-time now. ..you know?..

/CB: yeah/ it's gest- I'm *lonely*-it's not like y'kno', that's not, but that's something that- y'kow' that's something that goes with life. */ A:*   yeah../ y'know, it's not like-

A: Loneliness is not a bad thing. Unless you use it as an- y'know- It's not a negative. You know.. */CB:* yeah!/

A: (Continuing) .. right now you know it's not a negative. Right now, you know its uh- I have a *yearn..* for..for company.

/CB: yeah/ ...but, I think, you know, maybe *(clears throat/sighs),* maybe the inner self's saying, **"not yet."** *(Sighs)*

I think, you know maybe- *(horn sound)* maybe that's, you know it's not that I'm scare-. I've never had any problem before.

CB: well!~ I'm glad we had a chance to do this. *Quietly*

A: ... it was pretty good. *"*

CB: it's okay? *"*

A: yeah. I'm glad. *"*

CB: yeah. me too. so.. so 'll see how..how it is.. ahmm.. the message *I* got was it's been there all along! /... / *"*

A: (LOUD) Em-hymm, Oh yeah!! I well I- I think we all know, y'know the inner self is there all along. It's just we're not, smart enough to use it, I guess. I don't know it's-

C: yeah..

A: *{Breathing out with a Long sigh..}*

C: Well, any other thoughts on, this experience, or-

A: I think it's- y'know..I- I enjoyed it!! It's y'know it's..

Like I said, it just kind of like.. *(softly)* woke something up .. y'know..that was *there. (Louder:) Well I don't know, it's just that I, you know I think, I was in touch* I imagine since like last summer when I started to be by myself.

C: yeah

A: -and I was more in touch with myself you know, because I, I felt myself growing up a lot more. I'm not going out- it's like-

C: well you've been working on this path for /*A:* yeah/ a *long time..*

A: ..yeah, I think y'know. But it's nice to do this and be aware that, you know (steadily), that you gotta you know, it's not com-

A: *..it's not complete yet!* You know that, you know, y'kno' you're not.. like this..y'know..when you're getting there.. But it's good!

> { *On friendships, not dating in awhile, scares him he's not,*
> *but doesn't bother him, not the #1 problem ..*
> *lot of people can't handle straightforwardness. Etc. }*

1.5 minutes

C: Well.. well, when should we meet next?

A: I don't know, you want to do another month?

CB: yeah, on Tuesday?

A: oh G- I don't know..the Fourth of July is Tuesday right?

> { *Slowly set appt., explaining work schedule, asked my opinion*
> *on dating magazines, being physically fit, weight,*
> *cholesterol, cooking school, attitude adjustment classes }*

5 minutes

= *Set Appt. in five weeks, week after 4th of July* =

A: ,, all right! so we'll see you in five weeks. Take care.

CB: okay ..in five weeks, bye-bye.

"Do I have a Guardian Angel?" The Core's Response was a surprise, **Yes ~ I'm not part of his mother. I am a part of him.** *This facilitated a new, developed type of independence for him.*

The Inner core provided foundation for Armondo's growth over the next year and beyond.

216

July 11, 1989

Excerpts

{ About his 4th of July near his home,

" Almost a Riot-in-the-Park " }

A: By the Seven-Eleven, they were doing fireworks from the roof. They weren't going over there. ...

And then the sergeant comes in. And a quarter to 10, they closed the park, you know. ... And now it's a bad thing, because everybody starts yelling at him and everything, so he gets out of the car and says, "okay.. and now he's going to bring three or four paddy-wagons.. And you know, "we're going to give you a free ride to the 19th District.."

But meanwhile, you know, these people didn't care, now they're getting real vocal, you know, And there were 200 or 300 people in this park, okay? And they get a real vocal, and they're calling them nazis and people are yelling .. *"Tiananmen Square.."* and stuff.

But I don't get.. I mean, I remember the stuff when I was 18, 19.. ~ Well, it was 1968 .. I was in the middle of the Grant Park riot when I was 19. / *C:* .. it brought back memories .. / So..

A: .. Everybody started cheering, and..

Here comes the cop on the other side of the sidewalk, he's ready, he puts his helmet, he puts his riot helmet on.. this is stupid, there's gonna be no riot here, there's going to be no fighting. Just disperse. I know these people, they're my friends,.. he opens up the paddy wagon.

So everybody showed them that they live there .. so they can't tell them to leave. / *C:* So it's legal, if they live there?

A: yeah, how can they Kick you out of your own sidewalk, you know. They opened the paddy wagon for an hour. All the cops left, they left the paddy wagon there. The guys were going for a shift change. So everyone came into the park and lit the fireworks. ~

C: so it..twas truly ... Independence Day.

217

Want

Oh *(chuckle) ! Well you don't (chuckle) fight people*

to make them like you!! (chuckle)

<12>

Floretta

Everywhere

June 6th, 1989

She needs to c~ h~ a~ n~ g~ e.

Name	Age	Occupation	Inner contact	Prior therapy
Floretta	52	Clerical	6-06-89	5.5 months

*F*loretta was subject to severe stress
having no idea she was a doormat.

She suffered from a multitude of medical conditions.

Floretta was fully unaware she was overly accommodating. Once, she was accosted by fellow employees as she lay asleep in the luncheon rest area. They pierced her ears involuntarily and her ears later became infected.

She lodged no complaint to nor about them.

Her emotional aims and goals for therapy were to learn how to get people to *like* her better.

The physical pains and medical problems were so vast, she was impelled to take a leave of absence from work the last two months of the five-and-a-half months of therapy.

~

In therapy Floretta strongly desired to stay in the *Present--always!!* She vehemently held to a basic tenant: There were no relevant issues *at all* from her past. *"Move on. Move on."*

~

The Inner determined a very low self-esteem and traced her extreme accommodation to the *past,* a girlhood humiliation.

The Inner core adding,

She is extremely afraid of being disliked.

Question to Inner, "How can she make friends?"

The response supplied was mind-altering.

Therapist, *"Really?"* Response, *yes.*

To Floretta it made no sense.

Ultimately, Floretta needed to welcome her Inner spirit--which went wherever needed by others--to be with her*self* as well.

She believed she remembered *all* the hypnosis, of course *"just down and up the staircase."* As it turned out, once past the stairway, there was no recollection of hypnosis whatsoever.

Months later she heard the audio of the experience.

Floretta was dumbfounded, shocked, and surprised about the answers she ~ the Inner core ~ had given.

~

Her family, friends and Floretta reported a *"Total Personality Change."*

June 6, 1989

CB: ..handy-dandy, *two* mikes. We'll get *you*, and we'll get *me*. ..so. Well see ..see what it's like! I know you're saying 'it's okay but I usually get a little uncomfortable myself with tapes until a couple of minutes go by.. and, I get used to it..

F: oh.

CB:..so see how it is for you.

F: uh-hym.

CB: uhm.. so, especially if we're gonna do hypnosis..uh, today, that's why I- I'd like that.

F: ok how long will it last?

CB: the hypnosis?

F: yes

CB: It could be about um,once we get into it maybe 20 minutes? /ok,/..or so. /uh-hum./ Um the fir- The question is, what are the questions that *you* have, or what do you want to know from your*self*?..are there any thing in particular- ?

F: well just like I had ask you *before* .. uh I was trying to, um figure it out, um some things about myself ah. There are some time when some people say I'm bias to ____ ah what they call ah in other words, as someone else are ignor I wouldn't ignor.. sensitive something like that, I think that's what you would call I guess.

CB: so other people might say, "too sensitive" ..?

F: no, other people might say from here "don't worry about it" whereas I would take it a little further, you know.

/*CB:* and what do you want to know *about* that?/

-and I just wanted uh- I was tryin'to work on this my personality to the point where uh..uh I, where people would like me, better. ..you know.

CB: so it's like "what do you have to work on, where people would like you better?"

F: I don't know *(little laugh)*, that's what I was tryin'- it's my person*a*lity I *guess*. Or why I would be considerable more sensitive than a person, other person or a group of people, around me..

CB: okay. So issues of, "am I more sensitive? or *why* am I more sensitive?" or-

F: yeah right..*why* / *C:* -what do I have to work on-? / *why* do I ex- why do I uh I guess say worry about things,,that other people would *ig*nore, you know like I were tellin' you that my family probably would tell *me* that what I'm worrying about is not you know nothing to be worrying about, you know, whereas I don't see it like that.

CB: so you couldn't even *talk* to your family about this because they would..hold you in, lower esteem?, like it should, like it's all your problem .. you should be able to get along with people. like-

222

F: -yeah I worry about someone, that I were telling you I worry about my supervisor taryn my *papers* up, /*C:*yeah/ where they do other people, they *might* do other people like that and they would just *ig*nor it, and go on, and forget it whereas I wouldn't, *you* know. I would take it a little further than that /*C:*yeah-/ -so uh-

CB: -you would *act* on it-..?

F: if I would act on it I would feel *bad* about it.

CB: if you *did* act on it.

F: yeah I would still feel *bad*, you know, get *depressed* over it. And I was trying to work on not getting so *depressed* over certain things. You know. /*C:* yeah/

CB: so that would be another question about..*how* not to get depressed.. /*F:* right!/

-or despair?

/*C:* k, yeah!/ -because I had just looked at my writing, I had misspelled it / *(little laugh)* /, "desp-" instead of "depres-"

CB: oh yeah, the "d-e-s," des- yeah.

F: so I was wondering if.. if sometimes it's, *despair*? too, how much despair?

anyway I ah..

CB: So, the question i- /

F: I have to work on *that* because I don't want to have to go through these problems, anymore. I had gotten-you know-. My condition had gotten worse worse than I thought.

CB: while you were working at the-

F: yeah!, see because um it building up in-m'. You know.

/*C:* yeah/

F: so I had ah, with me being a'depressed as I were; I don't know how I could, work like that, you know in those condi- tion. /*C:* so you really- / So I don't want to get back to that, again, you

223

know I want some- I want some uh- I want to *learn* how to uh, not get in that predicamen' again.

CB: how'd you know how depressed you *were*?

F: will *now* I can think about it, and things that happen.

CB: ..looking back.

F: yeah and then I have a lot of papers at home.
  /*C:* okay well-/ I writes a lot of notes.

CB: yeah you have a lot to remind you.

F: yeah I keep a little..notebook, and I write notes.

CB: well being off, or taking off for two months, and feeling better, no more headaches, no more upset stomach-

F: well see my doctor- my medical doctor um physically is nothing wrong with me./*C:* yeah/ you know, my blood pressure's normal..and all of that, so. /*C:*yeah/ It's just emotional problem.

CB: are you feeling less depressed or um- ?

F: well now, because at that time I were depressed *all* the time.

CB: yeah. ..and now?/

F: but now *some* time it might come..if I think about some-thing..but if I stay busy.

CB: what happens when you think about going back to work? or *that* work.

F: well I feels if I'm going back to another department.

CB: okay so your..your game plan at this point is *not* to go back to that same job- /

F: or if I go there I won't be there *long*, jus' maybe a few days. / *CB:* ..once you know that the other thing's coming.

F: yeah.

CB: okay. So your..your question is ah about de*press*ion and um *worry*, and being *liked*, better, your *sensitivity*. Um, anything about..your family? I should mention that you..they're all, 'high *achievers'* and../

F: well *most* of 'em are..not all of em..most of 'em..

..one construction worker, and in' someone in the Dean's office? and uh he's director of personnel. /C: yeah/ Yeah, and my sister-in-law is in *Tennessee* now, she's workin' on her Ph.D. too, is why.. the one that work, workin' moveus.

CB: ..yeah she's working on her PhD. and.. *(talking together)* ?

/ *F:* yeah she'll be gettin' her Ph.D. this *sum*mer.

CB: ..and um.. you're like *one*- /

F: yeah am closer to Esth- as one- that's the faml- ..I *am* closer to *them* than the ah rest of 'em. I'm in *contact* with them at leas..two or three time a week.

CB: But I say *you're* a high achiever -you don't say that- but I know you have *three* jobs, and but you're missing the B.A. by um..six months.. you have a question about *that*?..about where to go with that..or *if* to go?

F: what? uh th-? Well *now* I can concentrate on me'more .. -you know because ah my *son* and *daugh*t'r is well takin' care o'.

CB: you can concen- ..*afford* to concentrate more on *you*./

F: I can concentrate on myself. / *(together)* yeah./ ..if I can get my mind off the *job* long enou'.

/ *CB:* okay. min- so "mind off the *job*.." um-/

F: -because I- see when I'm wrkin' I leaves-see you'kn- um. I understand that you're not supposed to leave work 'carry your problem from work *home*.. And anytime you do *that* some'n's *wrong!* And that's what I were doing, that I would- /C: yes for a year-/ that all day I'm thinkin' about the same thing all the *time*.

CB: Out of the 22 years that you *had* worked for how- ?

/ *F:* oh but that wa' that didn't happen to *that* th' umm! /

CB: ..for so, for how many years?

F: Um that just happen 'm since '85.

/ *CB:* okay..so about- /

..about three years. Before then I might have had lit' problems but nothin' *great*.

CB: There's another area that..that we talked about, today.. where you help everybody *else* in your family and they...and th'y an'... you don't get the help from *them*. You can't even tell them your pro'lems or they..uh *disgrace* you or feel disgraced because..you're not *allowed* to have any problems.

F: *(little laugh)* tha' ain' how I- they wern't disgrace me but I was ..I said that I wrdn't worried b' little things like that.

/ *CB:* you said disgraced about the divorce./

F: oh, I said that my mother would think that's a d- disgrace to get a divorce. That's the way uh- that's the way the people uh..the area that I liv- was raised around, that's the way they *feel*, they../*C:* yeah/..they think they you shouldn,,stay *together*, once you get *mar*ried.

CB: so they know now, after you waited a couple years and then told them, and, did they feel disgraced?

F: well....she still consider my ex-husband as my husband.

CB: so she doesn't believe in a di*vorce*..?

F: no, they don't believe- ther's a lot of people don't believe in divorce.s bec.. /*C:* so she's-/ My uncle tell me that he's still my responsi*bi*lite'.

CB: ..he's your responsibility even though- So he's not your *ex*-husband in *their* mind.

F: Right. He said that once you get *mar*ried in the sight of God, you're still married to this person. Even though you're divorced uh legally but.

CB: ..kind of..a strict Catholic?

F: They're *Bap*tists *(laughing)* but.

..but like a strict Catholic.

Yeah right. *(laughing)* They think that you're still re*spon*sible for 'im.

CB: ..Are strict Baptists like strict Catholics?

F: uh that's the way they feel, they're Baptists but that's the way they feel.

CB: ah.

F: He said in the *Bi*ble uh you're considered still divorced, I mean, still *mar*ried. In the sight of God you still- he said once you /C: yeah/ get married to someone even if you get married again that first marriag'...you're still...

CB: so the idea of..where the *fam*ily's at versus where *you*'re at and..and um..difficulty in talking to them. /F: well uh!/ about it..

F: I'm not *livin'* close around there for one thing. I have *friends* that I talk to. ..but my family's all ou' th' city. / -/ They don't live here in the *city*.

CB: ..let me ask you this..and then we can..go into..the hypnosis..i'y'like'. What do you think your relationship is right *now* with your inner self?

F: ..well..I'm not as unhappy with myself as I were *before*. You know before when I first start *comin'* here. Now I feel little more uh..um..at *peace* with myself, you know I'm not as unhap' at first I were really lookin' *down* on myself, you know like I exprs't- I explain that too because of the way that other people *treated* me, then it made me feel as'if something was *wrong* with me.

CB: ..so you were beatin' yourself up a little bit tow'-

F: yeah..I wer'- I were feeling as-f 's- There must be somethin' wrong for me to be *treated* like this, you know..for then' y'know I don't expect to b- except I found out that i' i' way down there *was* something wrong with me.

/ *C:* not the w- /

Because I was *let'n* them *do* that to me /*C:* yeah/ I shouldn't have let them *do* that to me. /*C:* yeah/

CB: ..so it wasn't that anything was *bad* with you..um /*F:*..no/ or *wrong* with you..it was that you..were putting *up* with a lot.

F: Yes I didn't know how to say "no" to nothin'.

But you know I wouldn't be able to uh..do that anymore. If I know that someone is /*CB:*yeah/ taking advantage of me well I know how to say no.

CB: well the trouble lately, the only trouble is, what to do when you face that..that origin'l *job*. um../

F: well you see for one thing the thing that I was acceptin' *before* I'm not going accept that any more. Like them puttin' me out of my craft to a lower job, and there our jobs in my craft *there*. You know I'm not going to *accept* that any more.

CB: So..the last two months..why would you say you stayed away?..from th-

F: From the job? Oh I w'rn't able to work.

CB: ..so it was a phys- at this point physical-

F: ..because *physically* I w'rn't able to work. The *head*aches wouldn't allow me to work. You know and then with my *stomach* being upset the way I were...

CB: Do you wanna know about that, should we ask about- should I ask about headaches? stomach aches on the job?

F: ..well, I feel the headaches were coming from the stress and tension that I were goin' under..after they didn't find any- thing physical..wrong with me, in fact that's what my doctor said, that it's from stress.

CB: I think he said that after you..after you worked on a lot of things here, about..medications..and all sorts of physical.. things; and then you were *also* pinning it down, to more stress..

/ F: yeah that's so../

CB:...than anything else..once you got off all those medications.

F: Oh yeah. Well see I- it was hard for me to determine when I were taken the meta-cation..because the medicine that I was takin' that's one reason why I couldn't say "no." Because you kno' like everything was *okay you* know..

CB: yea-

F: ..but then on the *inside* of me I was dep- getting depress'.

CB:..everything *wasn't* okay..

F: but uh.. I didn't kno' how-

CB: When you're de*pressed* it means things arn't okay out there..

F: Right. But then the medicine..when you're taking the medicine..medicine make you feel as if everything is okay.

CB: yeah..again confusing the issue, like your feeling it's *not* okay and you're 'st telling me it *is* okay.

F: well once the medicine wear off, then you get depress, you can think about it.

CB: Well shall we.. shall we uh.. do the..relaxation and the hypnosis? We have some *time*.

F: okay.

229

CB: ah..let's see here's a footstool..sit on this side?, /hyhym/ ..the hypnosis side. Excuse me.. *(moving microphone equipment),* is this your pen? */F:* yeah I think the white one./ okay.

Start by..putting your feet..what's comfortable..on the footstool. Getting comfortable..one arm resting on the arm of the couch *(siren noises)* ..the other arm- if it *feels* comfortable have the other arm- doesn't have to be perfectly even unless you *want it* to be ..and..taking a couple breaths *(fire engine horns)*..in and out *(more horn sounds!)*..just to kind of..relax *(horns, and therapist sniffing in and breathing out)* ..okay ..maybe this, this hand kind of resting../F:um hymm/ ..resting *there.* /okay./..that's good. And..whatever's comfortable. *(inaudible)* /okay/

Um..and..we'll..use the same approach we used before, the 1-2-3 */F:* okay./ *(therapist audible sniff in-sigh-breathe out)* ..How are you feeling now?

F: I feel relax.

C: Okay. I was just relaxing myself. I was really- I was a little tense here.. /F: uh-huh/ ..taking a breath *(therapist again sniffs in-holds-breathes out, siren and horn sounds diminishing)* ..breath out, okay..

Okay..so at- any other thoughts or feelings or? .. oh that's funny, previously "jittery," just looking at my notes when we did it one time..? /F: oh..yeah./ There was some jitteriness but better now./F:uh-hymm/..I̲ was just feeling jitteriness *(laughing).*

F: oh..yeah.. *(sounds relaxed)*

C: ..get rid of my own jitteri- jitteriness. *(train sounds)*

Well.. *(someone yawns)* *C:* Okay, I'm set, how are you?

F: I feel okay. *(sounds relaxed)*

C: Okay *(chuckle)* you're better than *me.* / F: (laugh) /

Okay..so.. at *"1"* looking up towards the top of your eye -thes' glasses ok, on? or off? /'k / 'k/ whatever's comf~table../um-h/..ok/

C: and then again if- if your hand needs to be in a fist, that's ok. Or make a- actually make a *fist*..you know, pretty tight, and then o-open them up if it feels ok../F:okay./ Okay..does it feel okay yet? /*F*: um-hymm / okay *(mutual chuckle)*, okay.

At "1" looking up toward the top of your eyebrows..and then towards the top of your head..up..while holding your eyes up..letting your eyes close slowly..your eyelids close while your eyelids are up..as you're taking a breath..as your breathing ..as your eyelids closing, closing..

take another breath and hold it..and "3", let the breath out, let the eyes relax and stay closed, and let the arm float up as the body's floating down..floating down.. The body's floating down as the arm's floating up..going in deeper..deeper to a relaxed..trance..place.

..relaxing..relaxing..breathing in, nurturing, relaxing..and then breathing it throughout..the being, throughout the body.

and breathing in..and breathing out. And again letting *your arm go. It has the* power..*to go up...and up it goes, and let it be..wherever it..wishes to be. As it was going up, it is going up, going deeper and deeper..re-l-a-x-e-d.*

And if y- Noticing the staircase *..the very uh..solid banister going* <u>down</u>. *You also notice another solid banister coming* <u>up</u>. *You see those solid banisters with that..very comfortable looking staircase, and it may have carpeting; it may be cover-ed. Uh is there- You may see a particular* color *on it at this point, you may not, but if you do see a particular color, 'to be a very..*enjoyable *color for you.*

Do you see a color? **yes.**

ok..what color?

brown.   *(or green?)*

ok. and it's a comfortable comforting staircase..and you're there on the staircase. 8 down to 7 going down the staircase, 10 times more relaxed. "And perhaps you might like to know where you at, in trance, where you'd like that to be at this particular time, and if that would be okay um, I'll count to 1-2-3. And at the word "state," a number will pop to mind from 1 to 100, the higher being the deepest trance state you can imagine, and 1 being the lightest, 50 being in the middle.

and see what number comes to mind .. 'nd you'll be able to say that number, and say the number, very easily and readily. 1-2-3-state!

*"**what number..**"*

a number pops to mind.

"ninde*"*

90?

"yes.*"*

ok...feeling deeply relaxed, going down the staircase..down the staircase from 7 to 6, at which point you notice *that it's a <u>circular</u> staircase, a round staircase that goes around and around and down. Very comfortable, very comfortably, it looks like a relaxing staircase. As you go down the staircase, <u>down</u> the staircase, when we get to the center of the bottom of the circular staircase, we'll be in touch with the <u>Inner</u>, the inner core.*

Going down the staircase, deeply relaxing from 7 to **6**, *continue breathing in relaxation, breathing it throughout the being, throughout the body.. now 6 to* **5**. *Deeply..relaxing.. relaxing..again (slight siren noises), 1-2-3-state!*

A number comes to mind and what number do you see?

"65."

*'k.. now going deeper and deeper..relaxing..down to **3**.. <u>down</u> that circular staircase ..and one more time, state!.. and what number..comes up?*

"40"

*okay just drifting and relaxing..breathing in comfort and nurturence..and now down to **2**.* (slight siren noises) *..deeper and deeply relaxed..**1**.* (mild siren contin.) *..<u>very</u> deeply relaxed..*

*And **0**.*   (quiet)

..very..very..relaxed...and let me know when the Inner is here,
I'D LIKE TO SPEAK WITH THE INNER.

17 seconds

AND..HELLO!
um-hym
(v quietly)

OK. ..NOW WHAT DO I CALL YOU?
8 seconds

my name .. my name is Floretta
OKAY. AND HOW LONG HAVE YOU BEEN..BEEN HERE?
in the office here?
SURE.

just about.. 30 minutes.

OKAY. HOW LONG HAVE YOU BEEN WITH FLORETTA?
10 seconds

i don't know

OKAY. IS SHE..IN..COMMUNICATION WITH YOU?

yes.

OKAY. ALL OF THE TIME OR SOME OF THE TIME?

some of the time.

OKAY. AND ARE YOU IN COMMUNICATION WITH HER?

yes!

'K. HOW MUCH OF THE TIME?

well almost all the time.

OKAY. HOW MUCH OF THE TIME IS SHE IN COMMUNICATION WITH YOU?

some of the time

OKAY. A LARGE PART OF THE TIME OR A SMALL PART OF THE TIME?

about half of the time

..HALF OF THE TIME, OKAY. ARE YOU..AWARE OF THE QUESTIONS SHE HAS ?

yes.

OKAY. ANY PARTICULAR QUESTION THAT..STANDS OUT?

several questions

OKAY. ..SHE WONDERS, FIRST OF ALL..WHY WHEN OTHER PEOPLE JUST FORGET.. FORGET IT, FORGET CERTAIN THINGS..WHY IS SHE MORE SENSITIVE UH..TO DOING SOMETHING..TO RESPONDING TO A LOT OF THINGS?

15 seconds

(3 beeps)

they dislike her

SO THEY DISLIKE HER? .. AND SHE'S VERY SENSITIVE TO THAT?

yes
                                                            (*sweetly*)
WHY DO THEY DISLIKE HER?

                                                        9 *seconds*

i don't know

OKAY. THEY..THEY JUST DISLIKE HER .. ALL OF THEM?

no .. some people

OKAY. WELL SHE WONDERS..WHAT YOU HAVE TO DO..WHAT DO YOU HAVE TO WORK ON IN YOUR OWN..PERSONALITY, TO BE LIKED BETTER?

*you have to **fight***

..YOU HAVE TO FIGHT...? ...TO BE LIKED BETTER.

yes.

SO SHE DOESN'T FIGHT ENOUGH?

no

OKAY. WHAT DOES SHE DO?

accept it

SHE JUST ACCEPTS...ACCEPTS IT.

um-hym

OKAY

..AND WHAT DO YOU THINK ABOUT THAT? ..HER ACCEPTING IT ..VERSUS FIGHTING - - - FOR IT.

she need to c~h~a~n~g~e

OKAY. WHAT TYPE OF CHANGE?

                                                        15 seconds

235

not too easener

CHANGE TO A JOB WHICH IS NOT SO EASY?

personality

OKAY, SHE NEEDS TO CHANGE HER PERSONALITY?

yes

..IN WHAT WAY?

18 seconds

..OR HOW? I SHOULD SAY.

38 seconds

she recvs too easa

..TOO EASY.. 'K. ..MAY I ASK WHY..WHY IS SHE TOO EASY?

afraid of being dislike.

SO SHE'S..TOO EASY BECAUSE SHE'S AFRAID OF BEING DISLIK'D..
AND ..SHES VERY AFRAID OF BEING DISLIKED?

yes.

..EXTREMELY?

she 'ys [70]

---

[70] *she is or she ' yes ... ?*   *4-28-2005*

OKAY, WHY IS SHE..SO..EXTREMELY AFRAID OF BEING DISLIKED?

she's afraid to say no.

*OKAY. WHAT DOES THIS GO BACK TO IN HER LIFE? ..WHEN SHE'S
SO AFRAID TO SAY NO..*

11 seconds

when she was a little gir'

HYMM.. HOW LITTLE?

little

VERY LITTLE..?

yes.

..BELOW AGE..10?

yes.

..'K. ..UH ..YOUNGER THAN AGE 6?

6 seconds

in school

IN SCHOOL. ..WHEN SHE FIRST STARTED IN SCHOOL..?

yes.

..AND..WHAT HAPPENED?..

she wa' disliked.

..WHO DISLIKED HER?

her cousin

..OH..WHA'..WHAT HAPPENED WITH HER COUSIN?

they was pretty

..OH.. ...THE COUSIN WAS PRETTY?

yes

'K. ..AND WHAT ABOUT..*FLORETTA?*

they say ~ she wasn't pretty

..UMH..

AND HOW DID *FLORETTA* F<u>EE</u>L ABOUT THAT?

she wanted to be like them

OH.. SO THEY SAID SHE WASN'T PRETTY.
AND SHE WANTED TO BE LIKE THEM.

(... *tears*)   ..THERE'S SOME SADNESS.
..A LOT OF SADNESS?

yes   (~ *Crying-in-the-voice*)

K. COULD YOU..TUNE IN TO THAT SADNESS..FOR..FOR THE
MOMENT.. AND.. WOULD THAT BE OKAY?

yes.   (*Strongly*)

OKAY

WHAT ABOUT LETTING..LETTING THE AWARENESS OF THAT
SADNESS.. BE THERE..AND..IT'S OKAY TO FEEL THAT..
TEARS ARE OKAY..

IS THAT'S, FEELING SOME SADNESS.. *yes* ..FOR FL<u>O</u>RET<u>T</u>A.
THOSE ARE.. TEARS OF SADNESS.. THAT FLORETTA F<u>E</u>LT ..THEN?

yes !

OKAY. DID SHE LET HERSELF .. K<u>N</u>OW ABOUT THAT SADNESS?

no !

OH-K. SO SHE..SHE DIDN'T K<u>N</u>OW THAT.
AND SO WHAT DID SHE DO INSTEAD?

nothin

-K. SO SHE- SHE WAS NOT AWARE OF THAT SADNESS.
BUT YOU A<u>R</u>E AWARE OF THAT

yes.

..SADNESS. 'K. IS IT OKAY..TO FEEL..SAD?

sometime

..SOMETIMES. WHAT ABOUT.. THAT TIME?

yes

O-KAY. AND..WHAT WAS THE S- WHAT IS THE SADNESS FOR?

..BACK THEN.

they dislike me

..SO THEY DIS- THEY DISLIKE YOU, AND THEY'RE PUTTING YOU DOWN FOR NOT BEING UH.. AS PRETTY?

yes

NOW LE' ME ASK THE INNER .. WHAT'S THE TRUTH TO THAT?

the truth

YES. WAS THE COUSIN ..PRETTIER?

yes *!*

'K. IN WHAT RESPECT?

they look different

OKAY.

SO THEY HAD A DIFFERENT..LOOK! ..

WAS FLORETTA PRETTY?

no

'M. HOW WAS SHE?

she look different

'MM. OH. SHE LOOKED DIFFERENT. DID SHE NOT LOOK PRETTY?

no

HOW..HOW WAS SHE..INSIDE?

quiet

..VERY QUIET.

yes

HOW WAS THE COUSIN..INSIDE?

they wasn't quiet

OKAY. AND HOW WAS THE COUSIN..OUTSIDE?

happy

'K. HAPPY AND NOT..NOT QUIET..INSIDE.

yes

WAS SHE HAPPY..INSIDE..THE COUSIN?

yes

AND HOW WAS FLORETTA..FEELING INSIDE?

sad

SAD..AND THIS WAS FIRST IN SCHOOL..WHEN FIRST IN SCHOOL. WHAT DOES THAT..LITTLE GIRL..NEED TO KNOW..ABOUT HERSELF?

i don't know

IS IT POSSIBLE SHE NEEDS TO KNOW SHE'S VERY BEAUTIFUL.. INSIDE..AND..THAT INNER BEAUTY..THE MORE SHE'S AWARE OF IT THE MORE IT COMES OUTSIDE..ANYWAY.

IS THAT POSSIBLE..TO KNOW? **yes..**

OKAY. WHAT IF WE TELL HER THAT? .. CAN WE TELL HER THAT?

yes ! *OKAY.* *(~fog horn 2 times)*

HOW LONG HAS THAT KIND OF FEELING B..BEEN WITH FLORETTA AS SHE'S BEEN GROWING UP?

.. long time

CAN WE LET HER KNOW THAT GOOD FEELING..ABOUT THE BEAUTY INSIDE HERSELF.. AND LET THAT BE WITH HER NOW FROM THEN ALL THE WAY UP UNTIL NOW? AND IN THE FUTURE.

WOULD THAT BE OKAY?

yes.

OKAY.

240

*I'D LIKE TO ASK YOU TOO, FOR THE OUTER FLORETTA: SHE WANTED
TO KNOW ABOUT..DEPRESSION, AND DESPAIR.
DO YOU HAVE ANY THOUGHTS ABOUT THAT?*

no

*OK, AND SHE ALSO WANTED TO KNOW..A LOT OF THINGS ABOUT THE
FAMILY. LET ME ASK YOU, WHAT- WHAT IS THE CAUSE OF-
WHAT WAS THE CAUSE OF HER DEPRESSION?*

12 seconds

how she's treated

OKAY, AND BY WHOM?

people she's around

.

*OKAY. AND AFTER THAT FIRST TIME IN SCHOOL, WHEN WAS THE
NEXT TIME? ..THAT SHE WAS TREATED BADLY.*

(fog horn..) **several time**

*OKAY, SEVERAL TIMES. (..fog horn)
IF SHE NEEDS TO KNOW THIS..OR IF WE..UM NEED TO KNOW THIS
A LITTLE LATER..CAN WE TALK..SOME MORE..ABOUT THIS?*

yes !

*IS THERE ANYTHING RIGHT NOW THAT YOU WOULD LIKE TO
TELL HER? IN TERMS OF..HER RELATIONSHIP WITH YOU.*

no

*OKAY. IF SHE WANTS TO KNOW SOMETHING FROM YOU..AH HOW..
DOES SHE GO ABOUT THAT? ..FINDING OUT.*

talk in

OKAY. TALK IN WHAT WAY?

20 seconds

i don't know

OK.   JUST TALKING ..TO YOU?..

yes.

..AND TALKING ..OUT HER PROBLEMS..TO OTHERS?

yes.

OK. AND TALKING IN THE OFFICE ..HERE AS WELL?

yes.   *OKAY.*

OK I'D LIKE TO ASK YOU WHERE..WHERE ARE YOU LOCATED..
*   WHERE ARE YOU ~ THE INNER?*

11 seconds

wherawas

..WHERE ARE YOU USUALLY..LOCATED?

movn

MOVING.. **everywhere yes.** *MOVING EVERYWHERE..*

..FROM WHERE TO WHERE..?

5 seconds

wheram lactic

10 seconds

FROM....? I'M SORRY. COULD YOU SAY THAT..AGAIN..? ((v quietly))

movin ..'k.. where I'm lactiv

MOVING AND... ?

8 seconds

..ACTIVE?   *0 seconds*

where i'm lack ted ! !

WHERE- WHERE YOU'RE?- **ym** *(whispered)* **t~td** *-YOU'RE LACKTED.*

yeas.

..UM.. SO WHERE YOU'R- ..WHERE IT'S ..LACKING ?

THAT'S WHERE YOU GO ?

yeas.

OKAY. ... AND..ARE YOU IN THE BODY ?   *2 seconds*

no

OK. WHERE ARE YOU..AH, IN TERMS OF THE BODY ?

8 seconds

m...s movin around

MOVING AROUND..

yeas   *OKAY.*

ARE YOU NEAR THE BODY, OR, AWAY FROM THE BODY ?

yeas *BOTH?*   *way't*   *AWAY.*

AWAY..AWAY FROM THE BODY. ..HOW FAR AWAY?

i don't know

*OKAY. BUT YOU'RE MOVING..WHERE..Y- ESPECIALLY WHERE IT'S
LACKING; THAT'S WHERE YOU MOVE TO..WHERE YOU'RE NEEDED ?*

yes where I'm lack-ted.

OK.. WHERE YOU'RE- *that's where I'm wanted.*

OKAY! SO WHERE YOU'RE WANTED IS WHERE YOU GO.

yeas.

OKAY. AND WANTED BY WHO ?

10 seconds

people.

OK. SO YOU'RE..REALLY HELPING OTHER PEOPLE.

OTHER PEOPLE IN YOUR FAMILY..IN THE FAMILY ?

no

NO.   OTHER PEOPLE.   ..W<u>H</u>ERE ?

people around me

OKAY.

..WELL WHAT ABOUT FLO<u>R</u>ETTA ?

WHAT ABOUT THE OUTER F<u>LO</u>RETTA?

..DO YOU MOVE WHERE S<u>HE</u> NEEDS YOU TO GO?   honk-honk

no   *20 seconds*   honk-honk

honk-honk

'K, WHY NOT?

i don't know

K.   ARE YOU- WOULD YOU BE WILLING TO..MOVE WHERE..S<u>HE</u> NEEDS YOU TO GO ?

yeas.

OK..THERE'S NO P<u>R</u>OBLEM WITH THAT.

OR.. <u>I</u>S THERE A PROBLEM WITH THAT ?

no.

HOW DO YOU KNOW WHERE SHE NEEDS YOU TO GO?

i don't know

HOW COULD SHE GET..HOW CAN YOU GET IN TOUCH WITH <u>HER</u>, AND SHE GET IN TOUCH WITH Y<u>OU</u>, BETTER, SO YOU'LL KNOW WHERE TO GO FOR <u>HER</u> AS WELL ?

..THAT FOR.. IS IT MORE IMPORTANT TO..GO WHERE S<u>HE</u> NEEDS YOU TO GO OR TO GO WHERE O<u>TH</u>ER PEOPLE NEED YOU TO GO?

i don't know   *(faint siren)*

OKAY.   IS IT..MORE IMPORTANT, WHERE OTHER PEOPLE NEED YOU TO GO RATHER THAN GOING WHERE S<u>HE</u> NEEDS YOU TO GO?

sometime   *(siren)*

244

K. *IS IT MORE IMPORTANT TO GO WHERE <u>SHE</u> NEEDS YOU TO GO*
RATHER THAN WHERE O<u>T</u>HER P<u>E</u>OPLE NEED YOU TO GO ?

11 seconds

i don't know

OKAY. WOULD IT BE OKAY..ANY OBJECTIONS..FOR YOU AND HER
TO COMMUNICATE..A BIT MORE..AH FROM TIME TO TIME OR MUCH
OF THE TIME..ABOUT..THAT VERY..QUESTION ?

yes.

O-K. AND..WE, CAN WE ALSO TALK AGAIN SOMETIME ?

yes.

OKAY.

WELL THANK YOU! TH'K YOU.

AND..WE'LL BE..FINDING OUT AND SEEING HOW YOU AND THE
OUTER FLORETTA ARE COMMUNICATING..ABOUT..HER..BEING
TAKEN CARE OF..TOO..MAYBE EVEN HER BEING TAKEN CARE
OF ONE. SO..THANK YOU.

..now just floating down..

yes.

..okay, letting yourself BE WHEREVER YOU WISH TO BE..
COMFORTABLY.. BEING WHERE YOU'D LIKE TO BE..
WHERE YOU'RE NEEDED AND..AND WANTED AND..
WHERE ITS BEST AND HEALTHIEST FOR YOU AND
FOR THE OUTER FLORETTA...TO BE.

Just now floating.. breathing in relaxation.. And now noticing
that circular staircase, and the up banister.. see that staircase
coming up..by the time you get to "4"..feeling..very..

{tape ends}

..5 feeling very good..by the time you get to "8" feeling very energized (breath) and assertive and..really very undepressed.. and 5 and 6, coming up 7..and 8.

"Three" with your eyes *closed* rolling up your *eyes*, making a fist with the hand that's *up*--gradually opening her eyes and letting your hand float back down as you're opening the fist.

CB: how are you feeling?

F: okay.

CB: any residual *tears*?

F: huh?

CB: I mean, any tears left?

F: nah..

CB: 'k. ..it seemed as you were wiping your eyes a little bit.. just now.

F: oh well I couldn't..hardly see.

CB: Oh that's what it was. okay. um..

F: When I wake up my eyes usually are..can't see good.

CB: ..yeah..so how are you..how are you feeling now? -guess we gotta..stop pretty soon..but-

-how was that experience for you?

F: ..it 's ok..

CB: ok ..any questions..or thoughts about it?

F: n o.. / C: 'ok well then- / ..not today..

CB: okay. so.. when should we meet?

F: well it seems like it's better for me to get here in the eve- nings, huh? .. I guess I alway get tied up in the daytime. something comes up. /C: ok/ I don't know how long I'll be taking this theriapy. But I'll try to go at ah one o'clock.

CB: oh yeah the uh..*physical* therapy..

F: yeah for my *leg*..

CB: yeah ..let's see

F: He might release me from it, because some of 'em I have to do for myself.

CB: ..what if we do next week at the same time?

F: okay, yeah.

CB: I think I'll still have that time (...) okay.
So do you remember everything that we did, or some things that we did..just now?

F: *every*thing ..

CB: ..is that a question, 'everything'..or statement?

F: noo..I hav- guess I have to get out of here..

CB: oh okay.

F: I just have slight..headache.

CB: oh..
..what's *that* about, the headache?

F: oh I guess um..maybe I sit- *(cough)*... sit in one place too long.

CB: well there are a lot of feelings that go way back, and..
..is it okay with you to *feel* some of them?

F: ..what you mean?

CB: ..to feel some of those feelings that go way back?

F: ..well I guess I feel 'em all the *time*.

CB: Okay so it's not- nothing new. It's..now you know where they *came* from.

4 seconds

F: ..well..not necessari'.

CB: ok. So it's not necessary in terms of..

247

F: I don't know where they come from.

CB: okay. ..Do you remember *any* of this in terms of going *way* back..to..first started school?

F: ......when I 'n school?

CB: yeah

F: yeas.

CB: ok..does that some familiar?

F: what?

CB: what we- what we ah- what was *talked* about?
                                    in..in trance?

6 seconds

F: I don't think that would have..I don't know if that would have anything to do was *now*. /C: well../ It might have something to do with uh..might have something to do with me trying to get *along* with people or something like *that* ..

CB: trying so hard..?

F: yeas.   / *C:* ..maybe *too* hard.

CB: ...well, the Inside has its ideas on it but the outside *you*.. You know the *you* needs to think that through, and feel that through..about what *you* think.

..and then kind of come to terms..with that.

(Elec. sound)

..so let me know how you're doin..

[Set plans -- realizing we had not asked about her lost keys.]

CB: Can you make an *Agreement* with the..the inner part of your*self* that..that it will help you find the keys?

F: Oh no *(laughing..)*, I'm not going to worry about the keys any more today, I've wasted too much time..I just going to have to-what I'm going to have to do is call her and have her meet my daughtr..someplace.

CB: oh and then..she'll handle it.

F: yeah. Court. My daughter will be back in town tonight.. and tomorrow.

CB: [*giving appointment slip*] Okay I'll see you soon, I'll see you next week.

F: well by then I hope I'll be *workin'*.

CB: okay. well.. June 13 at four.

..sorry I got to rush here. I'm 15 minutes into *his* time.

F: well that's s okay..we've been here..long time.

CB: So let me know ah..when we *meet*..how things are..or..

F: what? then next Tuesday at four, right..

CB: right / *F:* okay / okay. I'll see you..see you soon.

The Fourth Wave

" For it is not hidden from you

nor is it far off. "

Fourth Wave

Challenge

PART TWO

FOURTH WAVE

June 07 to September 12, 1989

Everything thus far was further challenged.

Would the Inner Core be reachable in everyone?

A spectrum of people became involved as they appeared.

Subjects were of varied multiple backgrounds, blue-collar, white-collar, no-collar, high~medium~low hypnotic abilities, younger or older, physically ill or healthy.

What is the reality of the Inner Core in difficult conditions? All situations were included to further an investigation of its veracity--as a concept, as an approach, as a reality.

There are many *"firsts"* in this Fourth Wave series.

Would this group of people provide continuing useful data and support for a greater awareness ~ for a *deeper psyche?*

In another context, might this offer proof of *soul?*

254

Fourth Wave

Explorers

1.	*Duality*	**Rupert** 33 *Regional Manager*
2.	*Disability*	*Sophia 29 Corporate Analyst*
3.	*Struggle*	*John 42 Vietnam Veteran*
4.	*Superstar*	*Jacki 30 Corporate Exec*
5.	*Enraged*	*Miriam 48 Unemployed*
6.	*Confused*	*Jasmine 36 Mail Handler*
7.	*Burned-out*	*Orville 34 Union Steward*
8.	*Alexithymic*	*Walter 61 Retired Engineer*
9.	*Self-doubt*	*Alyssa 29 MBA Student*
10.	*Drained*	*Evita 34 Housewife, Mother*
11.	*Drugged*	*Sabrina 33 Postal Worker*
12.	*Alienated*	*Gershom 63 Caseworker*

DUALITY
June 7, 1989

*R*ubert was not in therapy at all.

Instead, his reason for calling was a wrong number. He had dialed mine, looking to purchase an automobile, and for some reason we spoke for a little while anyway.

As we initially spoke, I wondered if there were a deeper or providential reason for his mistaken telephone call. After three months of calls from time to time, we did meet professionally.

His essential concern was a trauma, a physical attack upon him many years back in school, that left him bleeding, required months of hospitalizations and multiple operations, with a difficult recovery continuing to the day we met.

The sole reason for the attack was his walking out one door instead of another door.

He felt a great depression, anger and severe anxiety. There existed dual temperaments each with a specific name. These two personas or ego states--one of nice guy and the other more aggressive--were engaged in unending struggle.

Rupert held an absolute conviction. It *had* to be one over the other one. For fifteen long months, his burning question was, *"Which one is the crazy one?"*

The Inner identified itself as **No name**, was **There forever**, and easily answered Rupert's question,

"They are both crazy."

~

It advised, ***Relaxing into life day to day***. The next week Rupert reported, *"The table is turning; I feel pretty good about myself. It's really sort of strange."*

DISABILITY

June 15, 1989

Sophia felt a crippling lack of confidence.

She saw herself as *"stupid,"* and unable to make a decision-- despite a doctoral degree, a post-doctoral degree and a quick mind. Her considerable skills were being used against her.

Sophia vigorously denied a childhood cause for her perception, nor was there any other cause. She thought it was patently simple: she was innately dumb.

Nothing could be done to convince her otherwise.

All the therapists she had seen were inept and stupid as well, if they challenged her ill-conceived notion. Once again, this time with me, Sophia was ready to drop out of therapy.

In the nick of time, we attained contact with an Interself, and an Inner core. When asked, the core readily revised her perception.

It redefined the so-called stupidity into a clear *issue*, a subtle

" family rejection."

~

In contrast to all other input up until that moment, *this* idea was well-accepted by Sophia. After all, it did come from her own Self.

And it transformed her life. Her relationship with her inner core developed, and Sophia acquired the natural confidence she richly deserved.

STRUGGLE
June 21, 1989

*J*ohn had been struggling emotionally over decades.
His struggle would become more focussed.

During another hypnosis session with some encouragement, further contact was made with the Egg. This was not precisely the inner core, we had thought.

At home, as he slept or while he was awakening, John was confronted by a familial force, his late mother and sister together,

" *Choose life or choose death!* "

~

Hugging his inner child, remarkably he felt a peace and serenity.

John chose life.

This made the difference John had been seeking for so long. He felt better about himself; and he recalls this basic change to this very day.

A dramatic syncronicity in the outer real world, unfolded for John soon. There would be further steps, before completing the first contact with the Inner core more directly.

The same John G from the Second attempt, *The Egg.*

258

SUPERSTAR
June 21, 1989

*J*acqueline was a woman of culture and confidence.

A corporate executive, hard-working, energetic and attractive, she radiated a self-assurance. She had no problems with herself she knew of, nor held any concerns about her family of origin.

Jacki exuded confidence.

Based on her relationship with Robert, she gradually became involved in the therapy. And two months after he did, Jacqueline attempted contact with her own inner core.

In first seeking it, she viewed the core as *"miles and miles away."* She could not reach and did not see, the bottom of the staircase.

IS IT OKAY TO TALK DIRECTLY WITH THE CORE OR NOT?

"*I am.*"　　　　　was the response.

~

For a moment Jacki tapped into a *"peaceful and very powerful place,"* as a realization popped into her mind,
"I'm not always right."
Jacqueline back awake reported this as a flash of insight.

Two months later Jacki made further contact with the core, via a *"tube"* she visually devised. She described *"an incredible feeling of Strength ... Sureness ... and Clarity !"* Jacki added: previously she often had an image of being trapped and looking up.

Eight months after, she attained an extensive direct contact with the Inner core, with its eloquence and insight.

In completing therapy, Jacqueline asked, "Am I cured?"

I responded, "...you started out cured. Are you uncured?"

RAGE

June 30, 1989

Miriam was filled with great anger.

She was in the midst of a vengeful panic with a psychotic overtone. Her love relationship had just ended.

Feeling out of control and not knowing what to do, she called me. Two decades earlier, as a consultant to the Family Services Department, I had worked with her family and herself, after she had lost legal custody of her children.

Miriam was a low hypno-tizable person, who was against the idea of hypnosis; and also against any idea of spirituality.

The Inner core was asked in behalf of Miriam, how could she release her rage? and it responded,

" she needs to murder her depression."

~

Miriam struggled over whether or not to disregard the inner core. In hypnosis and while awake, she was encouraged to *Work Together.*

Two weeks later, Miriam reported a recovery. "No drinking; good sleeping ... life going smoothly and calmly."

She became interested in spiritual dimensions ~ in art too.

An extra bonus was the referral and general recovery of her daughter Wendy, who while in therapy the early nineties, found her own core. She reported her mother's rages ceased in 1989.

In recent years Miriam shared her art; and encouraged me,
"When are you going to get that book done?!"

CONFUSION

July 5, 1989

*J*asmine was a mentally disabled mail handler.

Her confusion was extreme. However, Jasmine became the first actively or floridly psychotic person to reach the Inner core.

Jasmine desired hypnosis for herself--and somehow proactively had sought me out. With the general backing of her longtime psychotherapist, we agreed to some short-term therapeutic hypnosis work together.

Despite an active psychosis the day of the attempt, the Inner core was not only reachable but also was quite sane, clear & wise.

Miraculously, it answered each of her general concerns, and in addition pointed out specific traumas, long forgotten and covered over with brush--the turmoil underlying her psychosis.

It took time to arrange, and a year later we were able to review with Jasmine and her therapist of fourteen years, the audio tapes of her contact with the Inner core.

The Inner core provided basic insights, data, explanations. Perhaps these were to be useful for therapy directions and greater understanding.

Whether Jasmine could recall some of it or not, we had indeed tapped into *her wisdom within.*

BURNOUT

July 5, 1989

Orville suffered from a post-manic burnout.

He was a postal employee and union steward who was off work a month due to emotional burnout. He was at that time not capable of insight.

This was the first core therapy with a completely new patient. Referral was made back to his HMO, and in the meantime three sessions were held.

Orville had had no prior therapy with me, and nevertheless, his response was excellent.

The Inner core responded to the dynamics of mania, utilizing the metaphor of a horse. After the hypnosis, Orville did not remember anything.

The next week, Orville brought up on his own, "*getting back up on a horse after falling–but not going so fast.*"

He realized a "connection" to his inner life. "I'm trying to listen to myself a lot more, to slow down, to see how I really feel--not just a cosmetic approach."

Orville's condition had frequently required hospitalization.

This time, he accepted the core's input, achieved a balance and returned to work with a bare minimum of outpatient therapy.

ALEXITHYMIA
July 28, 1989

W alter was alexithymic. He was not aware of
or could not express, inner experience.

Walter would never have set foot in a psychotherapy office. However, he was in a custody fight for his son, and was urged by his attorney to do a little therapy to help with his legal battle.

Walter had low hypnosis abilities. And he had a conviction, which he made known right away,

"*I don't believe in psychiatry. I don't believe in hypnosis.*"

He agreed to the process, but briefly. As I wrote in my notes, "*He'll do this* for his son *or* for me - *rather than for any inward conviction at all about this.*"

Walter so resisted the first attempt, that contact with the core was instead effectuated *without* hypnosis.

Some surprising and clear-cut inner responses, answered the unanswerable questions Walter had. There were tears too--and even this crying felt tolerable to him.

In three weeks, contact with the core was made with hypnosis. Both methods achieved *lexithymic* results, that is, meaningful contact with inner experience.

Walter remained alexithymic ~ but now with an opening. While maintaining his usual skepticism, he had to admit a credibility about one inner life .. his own.

This antecedes a new development, which would occur

July 1991 ~ approaching the core without hypnosis.

263

SELF-DOUBT
August 1, 1989

*A*lyssa would not have been possible to treat.
She was frankly phobic to therapy.

She was 29, highly independent, in business, and going for her Masters degree. This was the first core therapy with a new patient who was closed and reactive to counseling and therapy.

Alyssa desired treatment for a spastic colon she wanted *fixed!*, but by hypnosis alone. She reluctantly agreed to my asking about underlying reasons, only while in hypnosis, but she did not see any use to this all. She contended, there were *no* underlying reasons. A spastic colon is only that, a spastic colon.

Alyssa maintained her strong dogmatic preconceptions, and held completely to a remarkable lack of awareness.

The Inner core held no such restriction. Once reached ...

" I am there."

~

... it gave a far-reaching discourse on Alyssa's psychological and family issues. It explained Alyssa's distractibility: *when she does not listen to her core.*

And it disclosed the Core's location ...

" in her stomach, in her heart, in her head "

The core upon request suggested Alyssa talk out problems with her mother.

Alyssa's written feedback verified her Inner core's existence, and her basic surprise! about it.

She remained closed to psychotherapy and to such ideas. Diarrhea ceased, life improved.   *(Three sessions total.)*

DRAINED
August 16, 1989

E vita fervently believed nothing would change.
Life for her was bleek; devoid of hope, care and love.

Evita and her husband had been in an uncommonly slow-paced therapy for three years with me. Each partner would not ask, *why?*

Evita was passive, then explosive; an emotional doormat and a physical combatant. Evita's physical aggression toward her husband persisted. Both she and her husband were closed to any feedback or basically to any therapy. They were locked into denial and turmoil.

A year later, Evita came back for a session. Now this time, the hypnosis to reach an inner core was in play.

The Inner core was clear to Evita about her explosions,

" it has to do with all the criticism."

~

The Core honed in on her current family, and her childhood.

Evita afterwards excitedly described her inside experience,
"Colors !! Vivid psychedelic ones. Oranges, yellows, then blues and blacks, then green and yellow."

The following week, Evita again responded to her husband's critical provocations--this time instead of assaulting him, she called in the Chicago Police.

For three long years I had done all I could to help modify their ingrained long-term patterns, and with minimal success.

The Inner core made the difference. Change she could believe in.

It came from within herself.

DRUGGED
August 16, 1989

Sabrina was blatantly impulsive.

She was exquisitely reactive and unusually defensive, in a severe and hostile denial, especially about active long-standing and tightly held marijuana usage.

She could not discuss anything about it. Instead was anger.

As a mother and as a postal employee, all Sabrina felt was *Stress !* She resisted any attachments, openness, and any warmth or support of therapy.

This was an inner core attempt with a blatantly hostile patient. The Inner core sorted out Sabrina's situation and her..

"fear. panic. trauma."

~

Right after hypnosis, in therapeutic shock, Sabrina wrote,

" *I liked talking to my second person.*

Why is it that (I) react with my heart and

my second person reacts with my head. (or her head).

In Times of: Danger, Fear, Pressures to

the breaking Point, she and I come

together for a little while and act as one. "

~

So much for a "people-pleasing" theory of the phenomena, here.

Sabrina would initially have been pleased to disprove, not to verify nor to help prove, the existence of her Inner core.

ALIENATION
September 12, 1989

George was alienated from people, places and things. He was a *"stranger in a strange land."*

And he was fond of pointing it out, that this was the meaning of his Biblical name, Gershom.

George was as unusual as he was rare. He said what was on his mind; and he was a good man. At a primary level he had the sense of fairplay, organic rightful indignation when anything was wrong. He was emotionally labile, or not, and politically incorrect, always.

His highest aim, especially when in balance, was seeking truth.

A colleague from his agency says, "George was great, in a war of some kind, dealing with the Mystery of the unknown, the society at large, etc. Most in the office saw only the asocial part of him. He was eccentric, not that he did anything to hurt anybody, just, he was sometimes not particularly pleasant, to many of his coworkers.

"Most people couldn't see in him his personal form of greatness, and his sense of humor and loyalty. However he was loved by a few, for example one supervisor, who tolerated all of his eccentricities in the work setting, and admired his intermittent great insights."

Two friends twice took him to men's stores to buy clothes – and for a short while he looked "elegant" – then reacting oppositionally, he morphed back into his anti-establishment preferences.

"His parental script was powerful." He exuded a fierce devotion to his mother most of his life.

George loved discussing family scripts and psychodyamics. He came up with his own theories about his wards of the state: ".. *The greater the family psychopathology, the more the loyalty to parents,*" and thus, "*All children hold a Reconciliation fantasy, no matter how abusive the parents.*"

267

~

George believed any "quintessential excellence" and personal powers he at odd times felt, were an ego state--that of Lazer, his older deceased brother who passed on after graduate school.

George was enthralled with family and psychodynamics, and with hypnosis. He wanted to try it, and therefore we did. In attempting to reach his core, the process was at first confusing, his consciousness circumloquacious.

An intertwining of energies seemed extremely close to his core in some manner.

When we did get through, the Inner core pinpointed an early tragic loss of his four-year old brother, when George was two. His brother was crushed by a truck in front of him.

The core saw Gershom too as having died that day.

~

Over time the core clarified itself to be his inside power. As differentiated from Lazer, it was there wholly for Gershom.

~

In certain moments he began to understand: the Inner core is more than and beyond any ego state. It is a cosmic or spiritual energy more basic than any family member. Most of the time, however, George still maintained, gifted insights were those of Lazer.

That was George sometimes.

A tremendous humility.

○

<25>

Us

INTERBOOK

2010

.. What are we ?

.. Where are we ?

.. Who are we ?

If you see this box
this is a first-edition

Interbook

~

This is the Interface
between first book
and Nextbook.

~

Commentary.

IMPLICATIONS & REFLECTIONS

IMPLICATIONS & IMPRESSIONS
[Intentionally Blank?]

This is not a conclusion, only an Interbook of thoughts.

This page might have been left blank, to promote filling it in with the reader's own impressions, ideas and experiences.

You already have your own thoughts and reactions. Many people knew about this personally all along. Rather than now covering the whole picture from any one point of view, next is simply a schematic presentation, an outline.

I've been thinking about this for twenty years, and maybe more. Philosophers and theologians have pondered this over centuries, and recently a few psychologists, have considered it too.

We are now able to share specific multiple *experiences* of it.

Now how to do the impossible, to pull this together?

Let's begin with a few practical areas.

The next sections will take a brief technical look, first at Voices, second at Two Basic Modes of being, and third at Identifications: what or which does one think of as *Real Me*?

I.   ❀ *VOICES*

Good; not-so-good.

As you have seen or heard, we have the good or excellent voice within, shown herein as the inner core of consciousness. And nearly all people carry in some manner other voices as well, of their parents, and others.

To begin to understand these dynamics, we look into voices and consciousness types, and relate both to hypnosis abilities.

About one-third of all people possess high skills and abilities in hypnosis. One third have low skills, one third in the middle. Each third has its own cluster or type of consciousness.

The one third which we will call the Highs can readily and easily tune into inner voices.

The one-third who are low, the Lows, repress all their inner voices. Much inside is pushed and kept down, moreso than with the other two-thirds. The Lows *repress*. Highs *compartmentalize*.

The Lows are cognitive, more into thought than feeling; into doing over creativity. The Highs are the other way around. The one-third in the Middle may cycle between action and reflection, and are able to partly relate to the other two-thirds.

Misunderstanding and confusion is most likely when any one consciousness type is dealing with its opposite.

Hopefully, Lows may learn to understand the Highs, so their repression will less likely lead to oppression. And the Highs may learn to understand the Lows, so they can deal with them more effectively.

There is an element of Low and Middle consciousness, which may be astonishing, depending on one's sense of wonderment; and in any case, it is useful. And that is ...

... The two-thirds who think they do not or can not hear voices, easily *can!*–if assisted whilst in a visualization procedure as used for decades. Nearly everyone if properly encouraged, is able to access parental images and voices of prior time frames. [71]

Another area of consideration: all persons are influenced, and remain unaware they are tranced in negative ways. This is the prime mechanism in inter-generational abuse and neglect of children and of adult intimates. Lows are no more immune to such pathologies than are Highs or Mediums. This is the *scripted blueprint* of losing.

Two more twists and turns about hypnotic potential: the Highs given their flexible thinking, may be surprisingly stubborn; and Lows with their strongly held or rigid views, may also be suggestible.

Inside.

Overall and generally, the inside world is like the outside world. Good, not-so-good, ugly or mundane. This holds true with voices.

Innermost.

This is the soft, quiet and non-intrusive Inner Voice.

Now knowing more about it, this was also hidden in the premise of therapy, and underlying all good practice. Better understanding was sought from somewhere within; we knew not where nor how.

Not-so-good, or not-yet Enlightened.

This will be expanded in Nextbook, and begins next page.

---

[71] *When observing this procedure with Dr. Jerry White in Chicago, 1970, it at first appeared to be quite unusual. In the therapeutic environment, it becomes natural even ordinary, especially for those who enjoy its benefits.*

If one's prime focus is with the Innermost core, all of this may possibly feel alien; yet it is all-too-familiar for those who look around and see what can be out there.

As to *"not-good,"* therapists don't wish to be overly moralistic nor make value laden judgments toward people. All would agree however, there are negative, destructive actions or interactions in relationships, families, couples, cultures and societies.

These can be driven by "Scripts," that is--*Blueprints*, operating in mild, moderate or severe form to structure personal and social pathology. These are first, second or third degree.

Such blueprints are handed down through generations.

Enslaved aspects of the ego and repressed unconsciousness absorb negative scripts, as they are propagated, less knowingly or via histrionic actions and verbalization.

Multi-factorial mechanisms are physiological, neurological, nutritional, cultural, familial, psychological, and particularly by hypnotic entrancement and entrapment.

Pathology is caused or maintained by authoritarian nepotism; oppositionalism; compliant reactivity; and by the resentments.

Negative words are expressed outwardly and interactionally, emanating as well of course from the inside world.

According to our Inner core work, these darker forces or pesky voices do *not* exist at the deepest level of being.

Thankfully!

II.   ✿ *MODES*

Where are you?

To clarify: in which mode are you engaged, primarily and at any given time -- the Ego's or the Inner Core's?

Inner core, meaning Essence; however this may be called.

The Ego, meaning simple, naked or lost; by itself on its own.

Not to cast aspersion on ego altogether because first, the ego clinically and psychologically, is a mechanism to mediate inside and outside reality, as seen in conventional therapeutics.

Second, the healthy ego is not a bland undifferentiated ego mass, although it can be, in unhealthy families and people. More will be clarified in the future about Inner Core *within the ego* to enliven it.

Special note to Big egos: All is not lost here. You are necessary, you can be redeemed, and you just might be transformed.

In the next section, Who are you?, this will be clarified. Here, we focus on modes of life activity in which one is engaged.

Activity areas include,

>Conceptualization and thought about Self and Others.

>Relating in the Family, at Work and Elsewhere.

>Communicating with and raising Children.

>Therapeutic or Professional approach.

>Any Job interacting with Others.

>Men & Women relating, etc.

Primarily in life activities, are two modes of being. Secondarily, are healthy blends (or otherwise) relating to situational context.

Overside is a chart to begin to clarify these basic modes.

Comparisons.

Simple Ego	*Inner Core*
Puffed up .. *Inflation*	Balance
Losing air .. *Deflation*	Foundation
Outside	Inside
Action .. *Hyper, Hypo*	Purpose
Authority	Truth
Oppositionalism	
Compliance .. *victims*	Aware & awake
Oppression .. *vultures*	
Resentment	Seeing
Compliance to Dr.	Adherence to Plan
Therapeutic authority	Organic knowledge
Analysis, pathology	Psychointegration
Transference cure	Reality cure
Me .. *you!* *1 2 3 shift*	Me, Thee & We
Control, projection	Fair play, flow
Help-rejection	Embracing refined
complaining, denial	problem-solving
Maneuvers *Bait n switch*	Love for principled
defensive distortions	optimal solutions
Avoid .. *platitudes*	Engage
Polarize .. *Thought-stoppers*	Resolve
Distraction .. *yield to?*	Intention ~ *purify*
heteronomy	autonomy

III.   ✿ *IDENTITY*
                       Who are you?

Being in either mode, partly involve choice and intention. This is where identity *choice* plays a critical role.

It is true that certain blockages, hindrances, negative states, and script blueprints may get in the way; and these may need to be taken care of therapeutically and-or by self-reflection, while avoiding any counterproductive harsh judgments.

Whatever the process, the *intentions* one has and the *decision* one makes as far as self-identifications are crucial. To what, which or whom, are one's primary loyalties?

Simply put, is one--are you--loyal to the world, to the boss, to the loved one, to one's minister, priest, rabbi, imam or sheikh, more than you are to your Higher power, deepest Self?

With whom and what do you connect the most?

Do you see yourself as Ego without an inner core, as a man or woman without a soul? Even if you are wrapped up in simple ego, is this the real, the one, the only you?

One may need to work on understanding dimensions of script blueprints, rackets and maneuvers, abuse and neglect, attachment and enslavement, attention deficits and repressions.

But is all of this the real you; is *any* of this the *real you*, the authentic Self? How you answer this question is essential.

If you identify with ego, you say yes to your Ego, that is what you are, at least for now. If you identify with your abuser or your tormentor, if you say yes to him or her, that is who you are or will become, at least for the time being.

If you say yes to a parent, teacher, or leader who maltreats you, then that is who you are or will become, right now.

If you seek, connect or identify with your inner core or soul, that is who you essentially are, and who you will become.

The rest is commentary--critical yet secondary.

○

APPENDIX ~~ A PREVIEW
HUMAN NATURE & TRANSFORMATION

Schematic Preview
future editions

TREE OF LIFE

CANNIBALISTIC EGO

METAMORPHOSIS

TRANSFORMATION

R E T R O S P E C T I V E

JOURNEY TO DISCOVERY

In Memorium

Seymour Kempner

January 24, 1910 - November 17, 1948

Andrew Warschauer Brickman

December 15, 1955 - March 25, 1970

o

Kenneth Ingram Goldman

February 27, 1951 - October 22, 1990

Marc Andrew Flesch

June 29, 1974 - July 1, 1989

To Contact Kempner Books

www.kempnerbooks.com
1 877 213-8770

It is not hidden from you nor is it far off.
It is not in heaven that you should say,
  'Who will go up for us to heaven
    and fetch it down for us
    and cause us to hear it
    that we may do it?'

It is not beyond the sea that you say,
  'Who will go over the sea for us
    and fetch it for us
    and cause us to hear it
    that we may do it?'

This is exceedingly close to you,
    in your mouth, and in your heart,
    that you may do it.

Deuteronomy xxx

Proof

7955254R0
Made in the USA
Charleston, SC
25 April 2011